Cross out the plant that is **different** in eac

When you match objects, the objects look the same and the names also sound the same. Find matching objects around you and say their names aloud!

Read the name of each color aloud. Then draw a line from each color to the matching paint tube, and say the name again.

Red

Orange

Yellow

Green

Blue

TINKER TOWN COMMUNITY GARDEN

PRE-K · MATH · AGES 4–5

by Nathalie Le Du

illustrated by Les McClaine

educational consulting by Randi House

 Odd Dot · New York

Circle the plants that are the **same** in each row.

What makes these plants the same? Talk about your ideas with a friend or family member.

Look at each creature and say its color. Then color the creature next to it a **different** color. Last, say the name of the different color aloud.

The MotMots are spreading seeds. Draw a line along the same path where the group spread seeds.

Callie, Amelia, and Brian are playing follow-the-leader, and they have to copy each other's movements. Cross out the MotMot that is doing something **different** in each row.

Play follow-the-leader with your friends! Choose the leader and copy all the moves until someone makes a mistake. Take turns being the leader.

LET'S START! GATHER THESE TOOLS AND MATERIALS.

White paper

Red, yellow, and blue crayons

Washable paint

Paint brush

Construction paper

Glue or tape

Scissors
(with an adult's help)

LET'S TINKER!

Lay a piece of white paper in front of you. **Color** an area with your red crayon. Next, **color** on top of the same area with a yellow crayon. What color do you get? **Combine** your crayon colors to make different colors.

LET'S MAKE: MIRROR IMAGE BUTTERFLY!

1. **Fold** a piece of paper in half. Then **open** it up so it lies flat.

2. **Paint** half the body of a butterfly on one side of the paper.

3. Paint one wing of the butterfly on the same side.

4. Carefully **fold** your paper again, pressing the paint onto the other side.

5. Open the paper and paint antennae and eyes. Then let it dry.

Are the wings of the butterfly the same or different? Why?

LET'S ENGINEER!

Oh no! The squirrels got into Frank's flower patch and ate all the tulips.

How can the MotMots replace Frank's tulips to cheer him up?

Make or build tulips for Frank using your materials. **Do** your best to make them look just like the tulips in Frank's garden. When you are done, **compare** them to the picture. How are they the same? How are they different?

PROJECT 1: DONE!
Get your sticker!

Matching & Making Sets

Shape is the form of an object. For example, wheels have a round shape. Circle the blocks that are the **same shape** in each row.

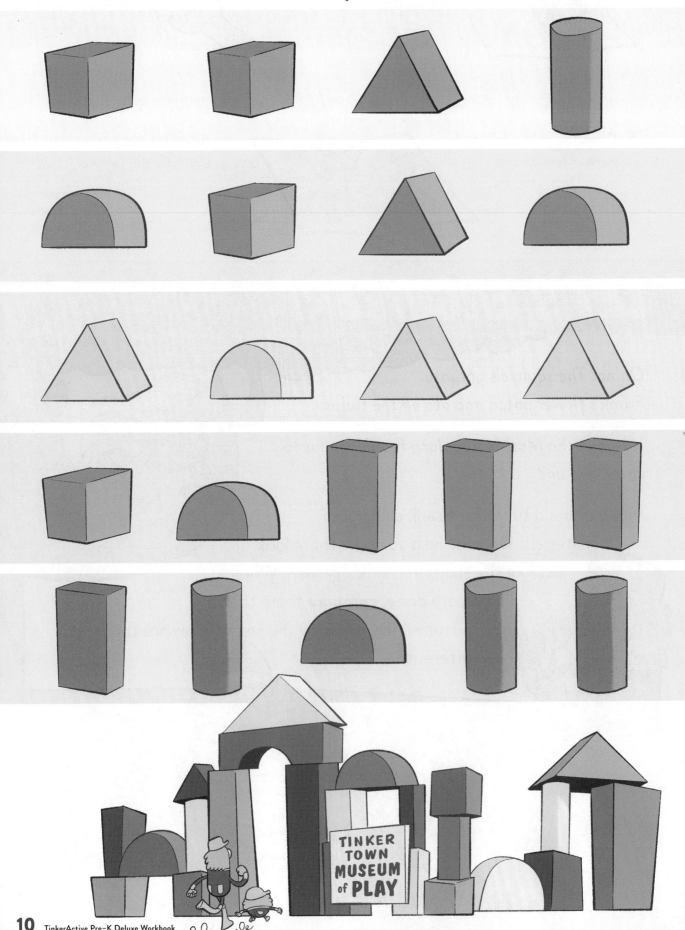

Size is how big an object is. For example, an ant is small and a car is large. Cross out the blocks that are **small** in each row.

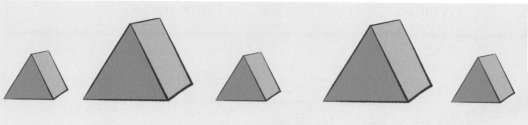

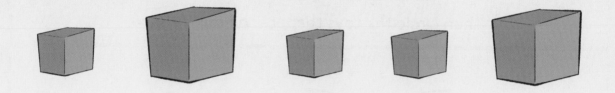

Circle the blocks that are **large** in each row.

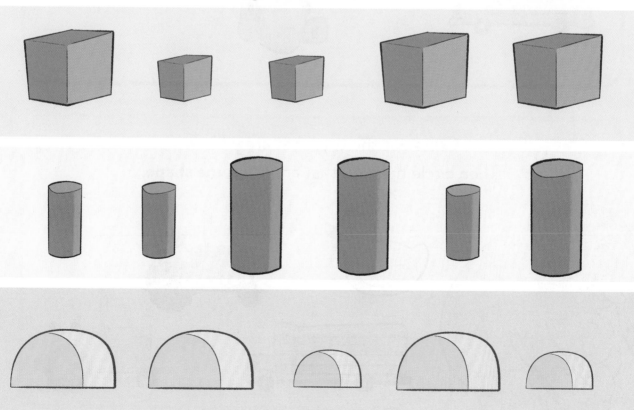

Follow the directions to sort the objects two ways.

Cross out the toys that are **red**.
Then circle the toys that are the **same shape**.

Cross out the toys that are **blue**.
Then circle the toys that are the **same shape**.

Cross out the toys that are **yellow**.
Then circle the toys that are the **same shape**.

Cross out the toys that are **orange**.
Then circle the toys that are **large**.

Cross out the toys that are **green**.
Then circle the toys that are **small**.

Cross out the toys that are **purple**.
Then circle the toys that are **large**.

After sorting, say these sentences aloud and fill in
the missing words: Some of these toys are the color
_____. And some of these toys are the same size.

It's time to clean up!
Draw a line from each
toy to the correct bin.

LARGE
TOYS

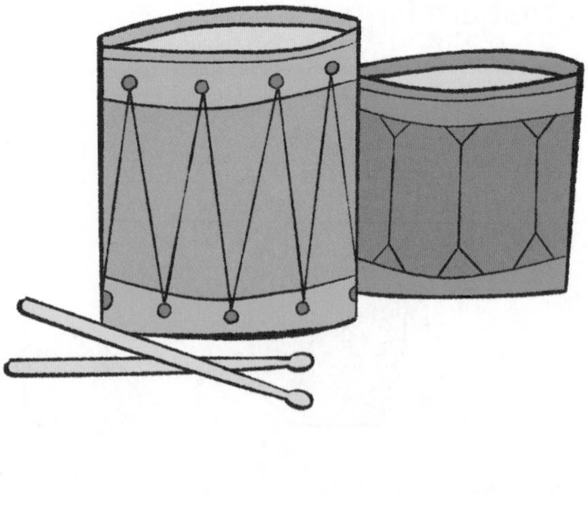

SMALL
TOYS

LET'S START!

Different colored blocks or small toys

Paper bags

Crayons or markers

Construction paper

Scissors (with an adult's help)

Glue or tape

LET'S TINKER!

Sort your materials two or more times: **Gather** your blocks or toys in a paper bag and shake them up. **Pull** out one item at a time, and sort each toy by its color. Now, **put** everything back in and sort the toys by their shapes. **Put** everything back in again and sort by their sizes. Are there any other ways you can sort the objects? **Make up** your own categories, like things that roll or stand.

LET'S MAKE: MATCHING MONSTERS!

1. Choose a few different colors of construction paper.

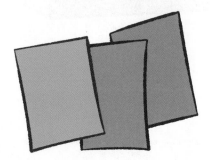

2. With the help of an adult, **cut** monster face shapes out of the paper, including a hole for the mouth. (The hole should be large enough to put a block or toy through it.)

3. Glue or tape each monster's face to the front of a paper bag.

4. With the help of an adult, **cut** a hole in the bag where the mouth goes.

5. Decorate each monster as you like.

6. Open the bags and stand them up on a flat surface. Fold over the top of each bag.

7. Feed the hungry monsters! **Pile up** your blocks or toys in front of your monsters. **Feed** each monster the color it likes to eat! Blue monsters like blue toys, red monsters like red toys, and so on.

LET'S ENGINEER!

The MotMots want to play dress-up, but the costume closet is a mess!

How can the MotMots sort the closet so everyone has a complete costume?

With the help of an adult, **look** in a closet or some drawers. Can you match a whole outfit for yourself from head to toe? **Explain** why the clothes belong together. Is it a costume or an outfit you can wear every day?

PROJECT 2: DONE!
Get your sticker!

LET'S LEARN ABOUT

Counting to 10

Follow the path from 1 to 5 with your finger and say each number aloud. Then draw a line from 1 to 5 to complete the picture.

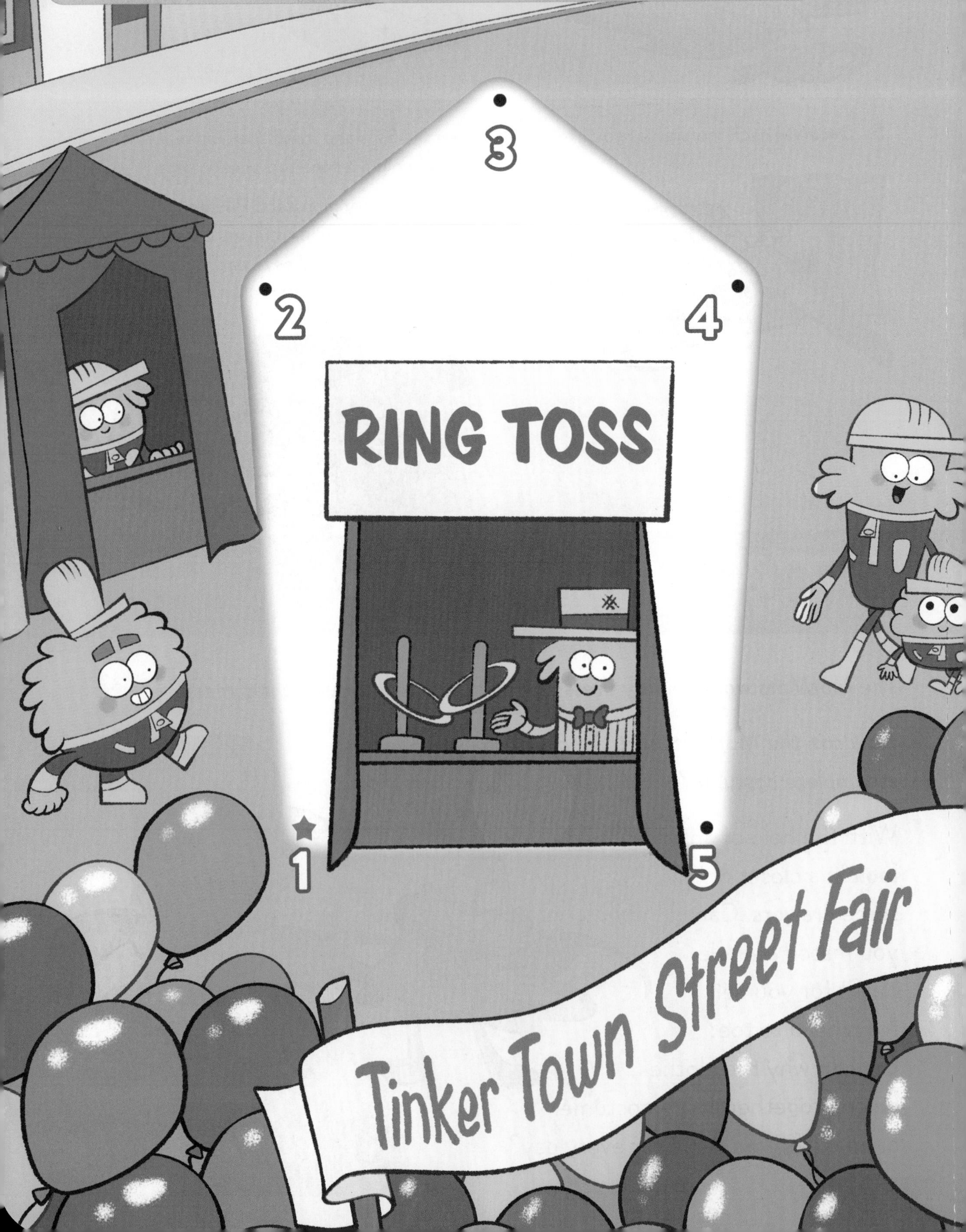
3
2
4
RING TOSS
1
5
Tinker Town Street Fair

Count how many fingers each MotMot is holding up.
Then trace the number.

0

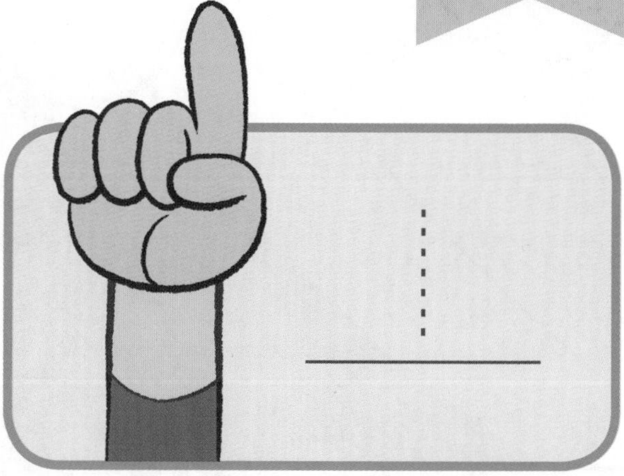

1

2

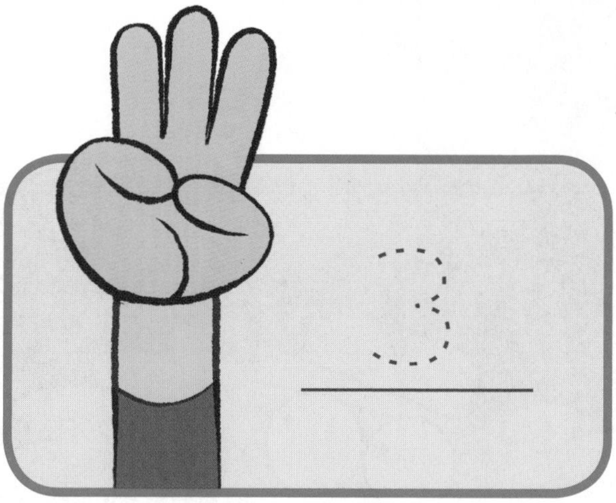

3

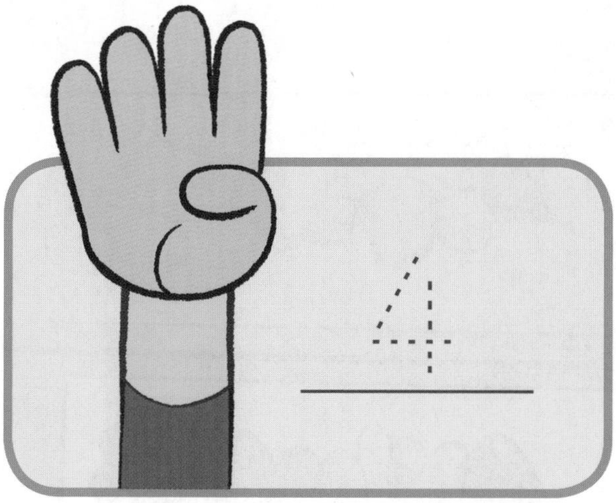

4

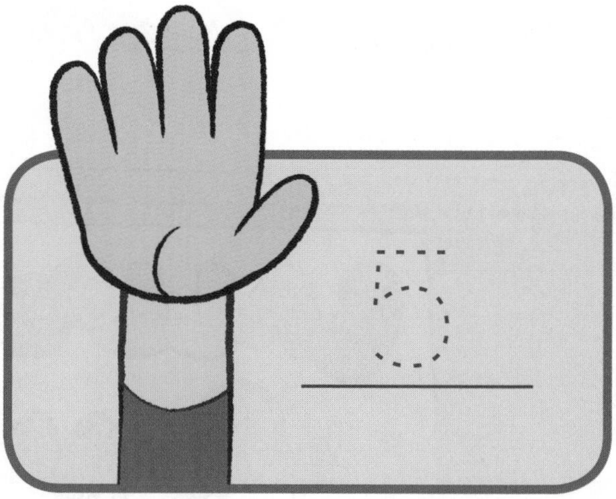

5

Follow the path from 0 to 10 with your finger and say each number aloud. Then draw a line from 0 to 10 to complete the picture.

Count how many fingers each MotMot is holding up.
Then trace the number.

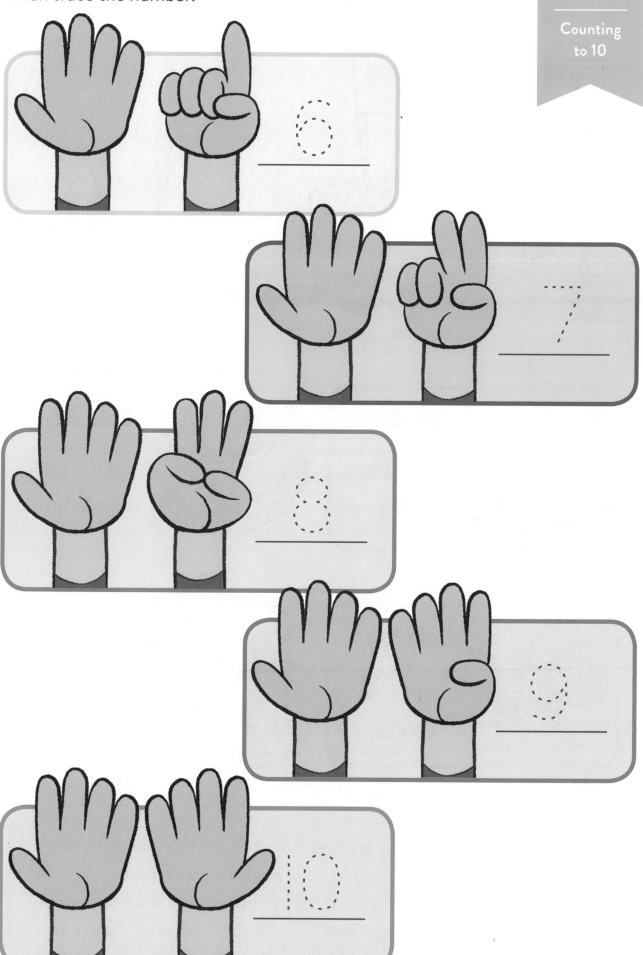

The MotMots are playing Enid Says Count Aloud! Play along with them by following each direction and counting aloud.

Enid Says:
Touch your nose **5** times.

Enid Says:
Touch your toes **3** times.

Enid Says:
Jump **8** times.

Enid Says:
Stomp your feet **10** times.

Play your own game of Enid Says Count Aloud! Get some friends and choose a leader. The leader says what the other players must do and how many times they must do it. But only follow commands that begin with the words "Enid Says." Listen carefully! If you do an action without the leader saying "Enid Says," you're out!

Look at the key, and color the MotMots by matching each number to a color.

0 = **red**

1 = **orange**

2 = yellow

3 = **green**

4 = yellow-green

5 = **blue**

6 = **brown**

7 = **purple**

8 = **teal**

9 = **pink**

10= **black**

LET'S START!

10 paper cups

Crayons

55 small snacks, like:
cereal, nuts, raisins, mini pretzels, etc.

Markers

Pencil

White paper

Scissors
(with an adult's help)

Craft sticks

Glue or tape

Empty egg carton

LET'S TINKER!

Put 10 paper cups in front of you. With the help of an adult, **write** a number from 1 to 10 on each cup. **Mix up** your cups. Can you put them back in order from 1 to 10? How about from 10 to 1? Can you fill each cup with the correct number of snacks? When you are done, **open** your own snack stand and sell your snacks!

FRANK'S LEMONADE

LET'S MAKE: COUNTING PUZZLE!

1. **Create** a drawing on a horizontal piece of paper using your crayons.

2. With the help of an adult, **draw** 10 straight lines from top to bottom using a pencil.

3. Number each section of your drawing from 0 to 10 using a pencil.

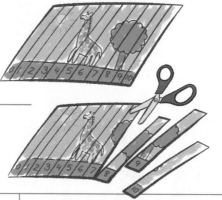

4. With the help of an adult, **cut** the drawing along each line.

5. Mix up the pieces of paper so they are out of order.

6. Reveal your picture again by putting the numbered pieces of paper in order!

LET'S ENGINEER!

The night before Tinker Town's street fair, a windstorm hit the town and blew away all the street signs! No one will be able to find their way from the beginning of the street fair at 1st Street to the end at 10th Street.

How can the MotMots help everyone know which is 1st Street, 2nd Street, 3rd Street, and so on?

Build your own street signs using your materials. **Number** your signs and put them in the correct order. You can also **draw** your own map of Tinker Town and put your street signs on top of your drawing!

PROJECT 3: DONE!
Get your sticker!

Quantities 0–5 & Writing 0–5

Count how many pieces of fruit are in each basket. Then write the total number in each basket.

Hint! You can cross out each piece of fruit as you count so you don't count anything twice.

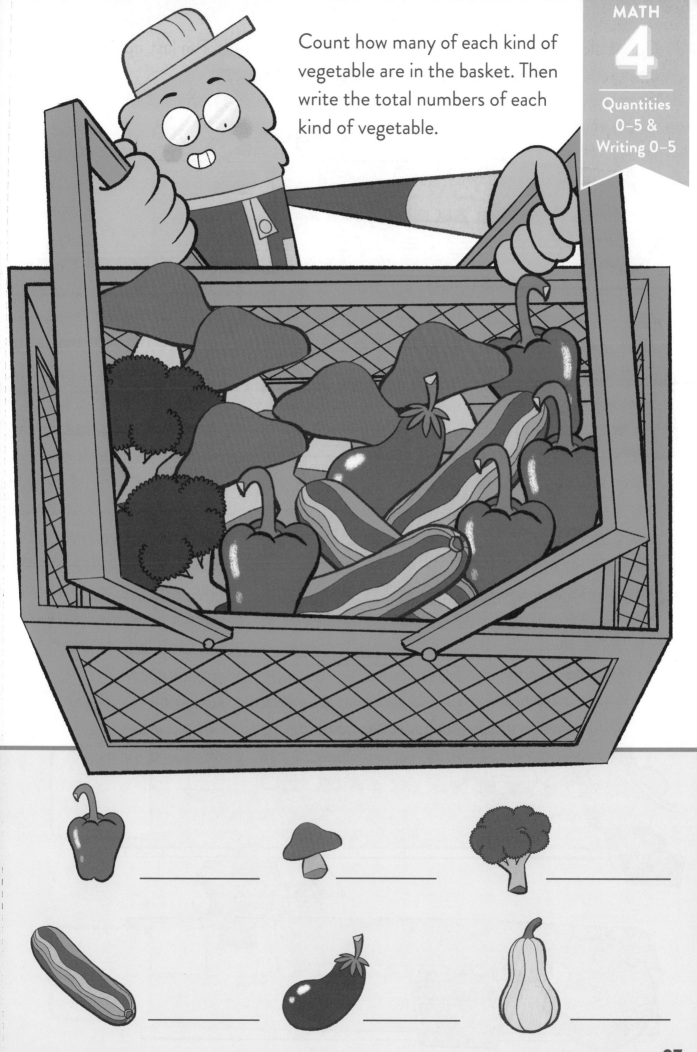

Count how many of each kind of vegetable are in the basket. Then write the total numbers of each kind of vegetable.

MATH

4

Quantities
0–5 &
Writing 0–5

Count aloud how many items are in each checkout aisle. The last number you say is the number of objects in the group! Write the total number of items.

Read the poems aloud to count each group. Then write the number of items in the group.

I count **1** and **2**.

I count _____ stews.

I count **1**, **2**, and **3**.

I count _____ bags of frozen peas.

I count **1**, **2**, **3**, and **4**.

I count _____ pears in the store.

I count _____ cinnamon bun.
Counting food is a lot of fun!

Can you make your own poems to count up to 5?

With the help of an adult, cut out the items below the baskets. Then sort them into groups. How many of each item do you have? Match the number of items to the correct basket by placing the items on top.

The MotMots are buying food for a party! Count the number of items each MotMot wants to buy. Then write the number on the cart.

LET'S START!

GATHER THESE TOOLS AND MATERIALS.

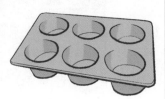

Muffin tin

A few groups of 1 to 5 small objects, such as:
beans, coins, buttons, etc.

Paper plate

Sliced bread

Butter knife
(with an adult's help)

Banana

Raisins

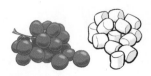

Peanut butter

Marshmallows or grapes

Toothpicks

LET'S TINKER!

Sort your small items into separate spaces of your muffin tin. **Group** the objects that are alike, and then count each group. How many of each item do you have? Are there any other ways you can sort the objects? If so, **sort** them into new groups and count them again!

LET'S MAKE: EDIBLE ART!

1. With the help of an adult, **cut** 1 piece of bread in a curved line.

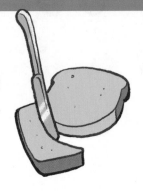

2. With the help of an adult, **cut** out a small circle from another slice of bread, and then cut that circle in half.

3. Get another slice of bread and spread peanut butter on all the pieces.

4. Assemble the pieces into the shape of a monkey's face on your paper plate. **Place** the curved piece on the bottom of the face, and add the half-circle ears to the sides of the face.

5. With the help of an adult, **cut** four rounds of banana, and cut one of those rounds in half.

6. Add the banana pieces and raisins to make ears, eyes, a nose, and a mouth. Then **enjoy** your edible art!

LET'S ENGINEER!

The MotMots love to build towers all the time—even during snack time! But they only have soft marshmallows and round grapes for snack time today.

How can the MotMots build a tower using their snacks?

Look at your materials. **Think** of a way to build something using the marshmallows that are soft and wobbly, or the grapes that might roll away. How might you keep the snacks steady? How might you build a strong structure?

PROJECT 4: DONE!
Get your sticker!

Counting to 20

Follow the path from 0 to 15 with your finger and say each number aloud. Then draw a line from 0 to 15.

Count aloud how many animals or objects are in each group. Then trace the number.

11 pigs

12 hens

13 eggs

14 mice

15 chicks

Follow the path from 0 to 20 with your finger and say each number aloud. Then draw a line from 0 to 20.

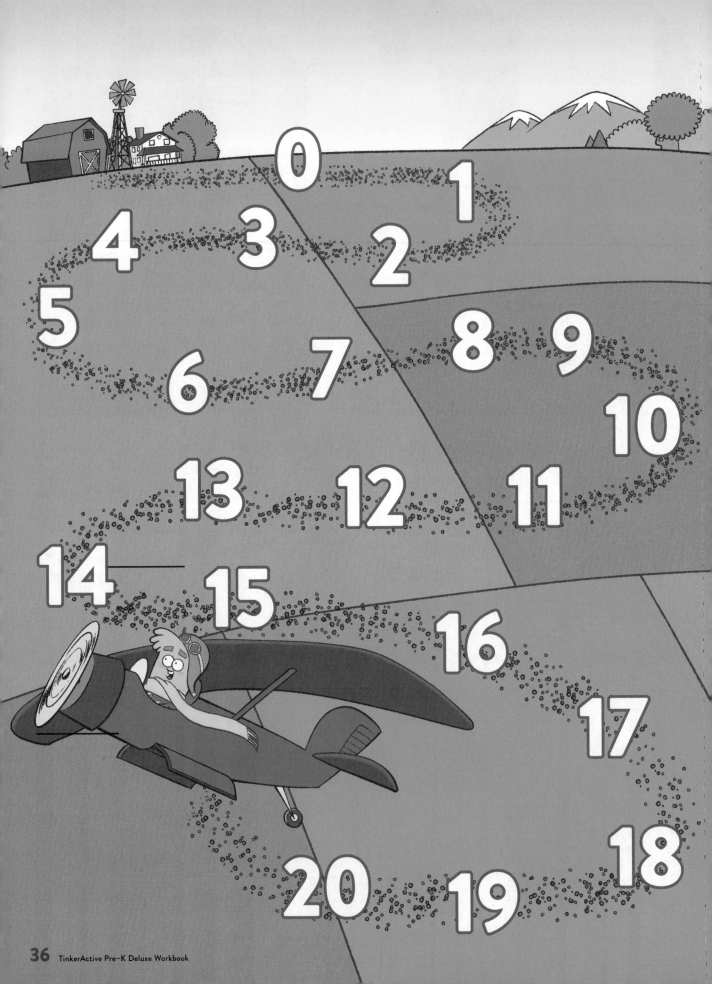

Count how many objects are in each group. Then trace the number.

16

17

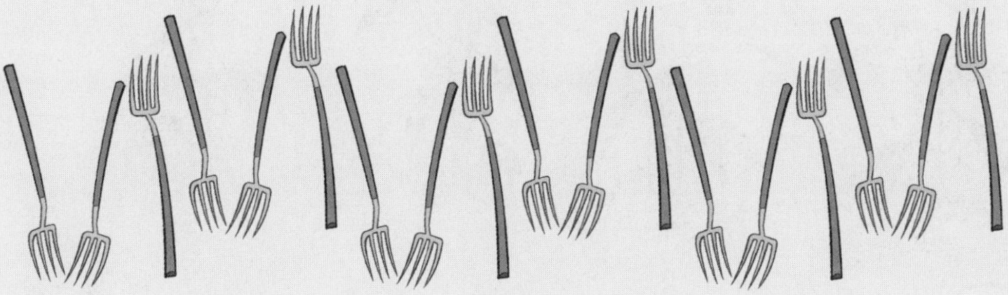

18

19

20

Enid loves eating beans. She loves them so much that she planted 19 different bean plants! Follow the path from 0 to 19 with your finger. Then draw a line from 0 to 19 to connect the bean plants.

If Enid planted 1 more bean plant, how many plants would she have?

Color in the correct number of stalls.

11

8

16

19

LET'S START!

GATHER THESE TOOLS AND MATERIALS.

 20 rocks

 Permanent marker (with an adult's help)

 Scissors (with an adult's help)

 Construction paper, including black

 Glue

 White washable paint

 Shallow paper bowl or cup

 White and black crayons or googly eyes

 A few toys or figurines

 20 or more craft sticks

 Modeling clay

LET'S TINKER!

Make stepping-stones with your materials. With the help of an adult, **write** the numbers 1 through 20 on your rocks with a permanent marker.
Line up your rocks from 1 through 20 like stepping stones—walk across them if they are large enough, or use your fingers to walk across them if they are small. Every time you step, **count** aloud. Now, **make** a new path in a different shape, without changing the rocks' order.
Can you count down and walk from 20 to 1?

LET'S MAKE: COUNTING SHEEP!

1. With the help of an adult, **cut out** 4 strips of black construction paper for the sheep's legs, as well as a sheep head and tail.

2. Glue the sheep's legs as shown on colored construction paper.

3. Pour a small amount of white paint into a shallow bowl or cup.

4. Dip your thumb into the white paint and make 20 thumbprints for the sheep's body. **Count** your thumbprints aloud.

5. After the paint dries, **glue** on the face, tail, and googly eyes if you are using them. If you are not using googly eyes, **draw** the eyes.

LET'S ENGINEER!

The baby goats at the farm keep running away and getting into trouble!

How can the MotMots keep the goats safely in one area?

Imagine that your toys or figurines are goats. **Build** something to keep them in one area using 20 craft sticks and your other materials. **Count** your craft sticks aloud as you use them.

PROJECT 5: DONE!
Get your sticker!

Quantities to 10 & Writing 6–10

Count how many mountain animals are in each group. Then write the total number of animals in each group. (Hint: You can cross out each animal as you count so you don't count any twice.)

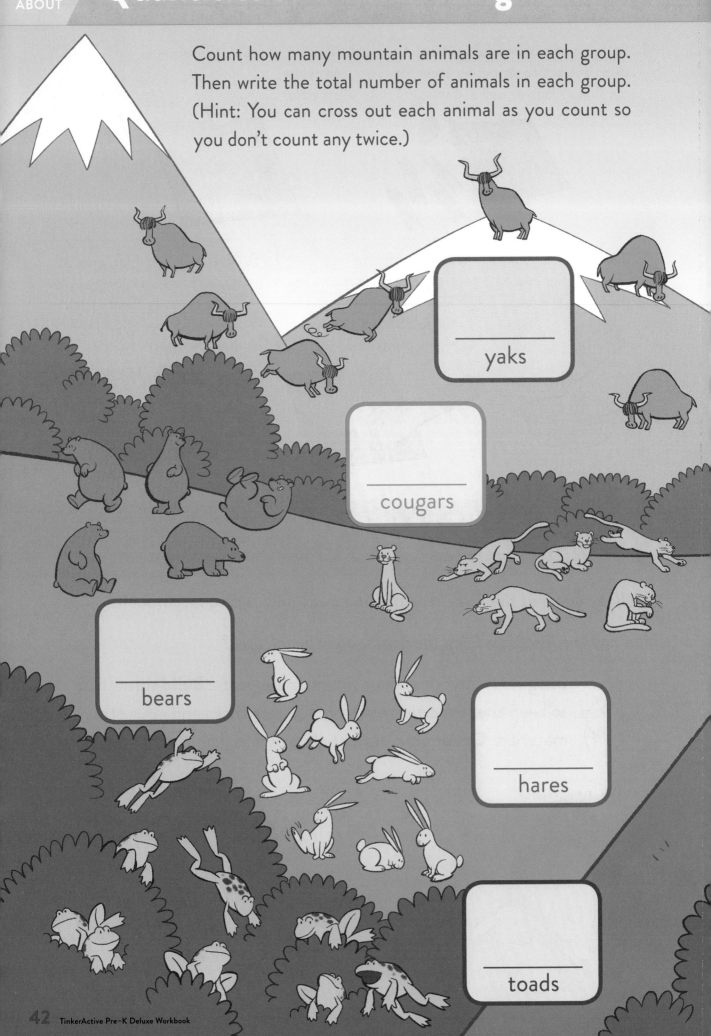

_____ yaks

_____ cougars

_____ bears

_____ hares

_____ toads

_____ hawks

_____ woodpeckers

_____ owls

_____ tanagers

_____ chickadees

With the help of an adult, fill in the correct answers.

Me By-the-Numbers

My name is _____ .

I am _____ years old.

I can't wait to become _____ years old.

There are _____ letters in my name.

I have _____ pets.

My lucky number is _____ .

I can count up to _____ .

I have _____ siblings.

This is a drawing of me:

I have _____ fingers.

I have _____ eyes.

I have _____ toes.

Frank is having a picnic for his friends! Read Frank's menu and use the stickers from page 385 to add the correct amount of food for the picnic.

6

7

10

Draw a line through the maze so that each MotMot collects the correct number of objects on their hike.

Dimitri wants to collect **9** leaves.

Callie wants to collect **8** acorns.

Enid wants to collect **10** sticks.

LET'S START!

GATHER THESE TOOLS AND MATERIALS.

10 paper cups

Marker

10 groups of small items, such as: dice, pretzels, popcorn, etc.

Graham crackers

Plate

Chocolate

Marshmallows

Toothpicks or wooden skewers

Aluminum foil

String

Small figurines

LET'S TINKER!

Turn your paper cups upside down to make "mountains." With the help of an adult, **write** a number from 1 to 10 on each cup. **Separate** your small items into different groups by type and count how many items are in each group. **Match** the grouped items with the number on a cup. **Try** to balance the objects on top of your mountains.

LET'S MAKE: S'MORES!

1. Break a graham cracker into 2 pieces and lay the pieces on a plate.

2. Top 1 cracker with a square of chocolate.

3. Top the chocolate with a marshmallow. With the help of an adult, **put** your s'more into an oven or microwave if you would like it heated up.

4. Top with the other graham cracker, press down slightly like a sandwich, and enjoy!

How many ingredients did you use? How many layers are in the s'more? How many s'mores did you make?

LET'S ENGINEER!

The MotMots were hiking when the wind turned and blew a rainstorm right into Mount Ten! Now they need to take shelter, but there are no caves in sight. They only have sticks, rope, a tarp, and the trees around them.

How can the MotMots stay dry?

Build a mini shelter. What are some materials that are like a tarp and might help cover your figurines so they stay dry? When you are done, **count** how many materials you used for your shelter.

PROJECT 6: DONE!
Get your sticker!

Number Sense

Write the missing numbers on each number line. Then say each number in the line aloud.

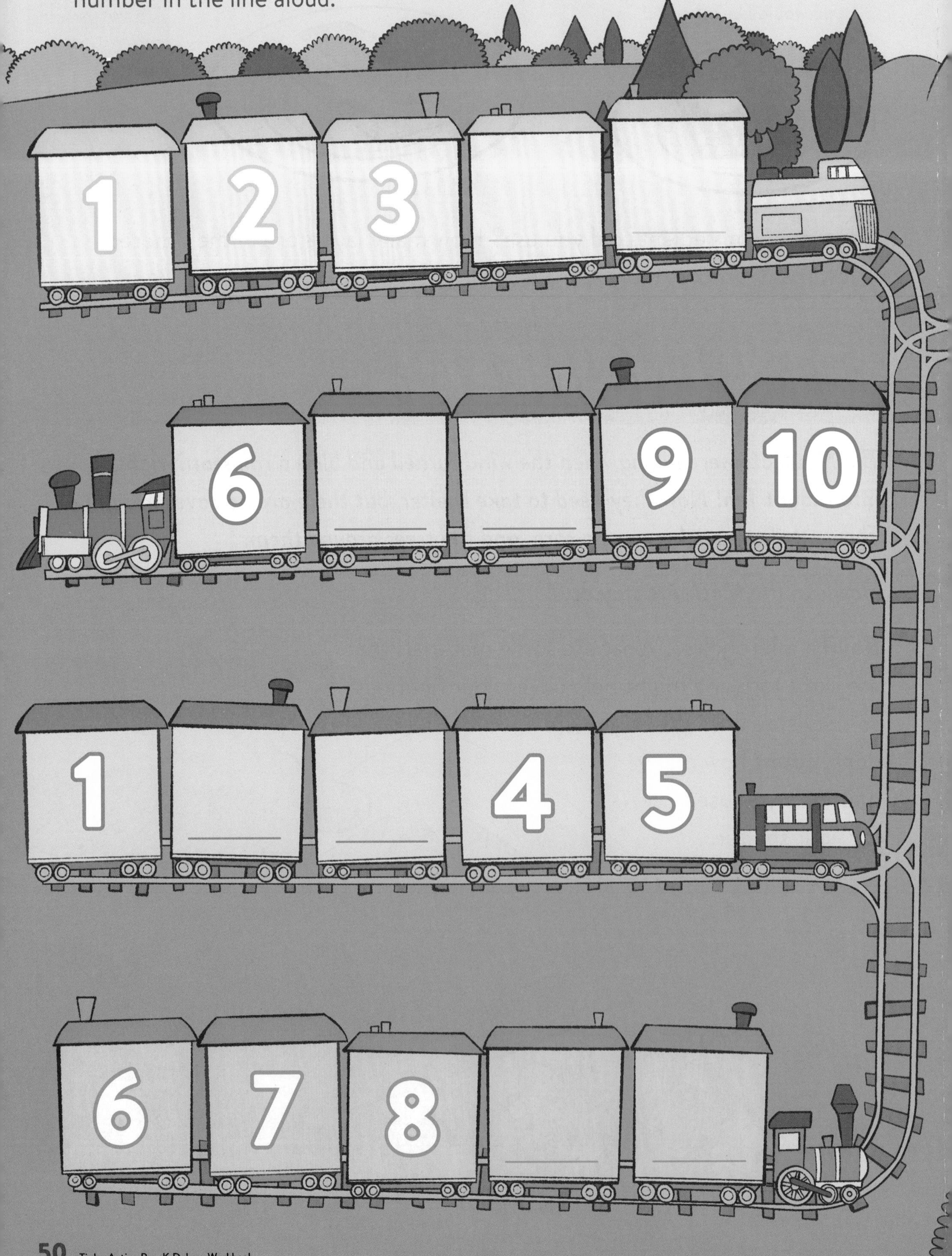

1 2 3 ___ ___

6 ___ ___ 9 10

1 ___ ___ 4 5

6 7 8 ___ ___

Complete the picture by drawing a line from each starting number
★ to 10. Say each number aloud as you go.

Count how many trains are in each group.
Then write the number.

3

Read the number and look at the object. Then sticker the same number of objects along the railroad tracks.

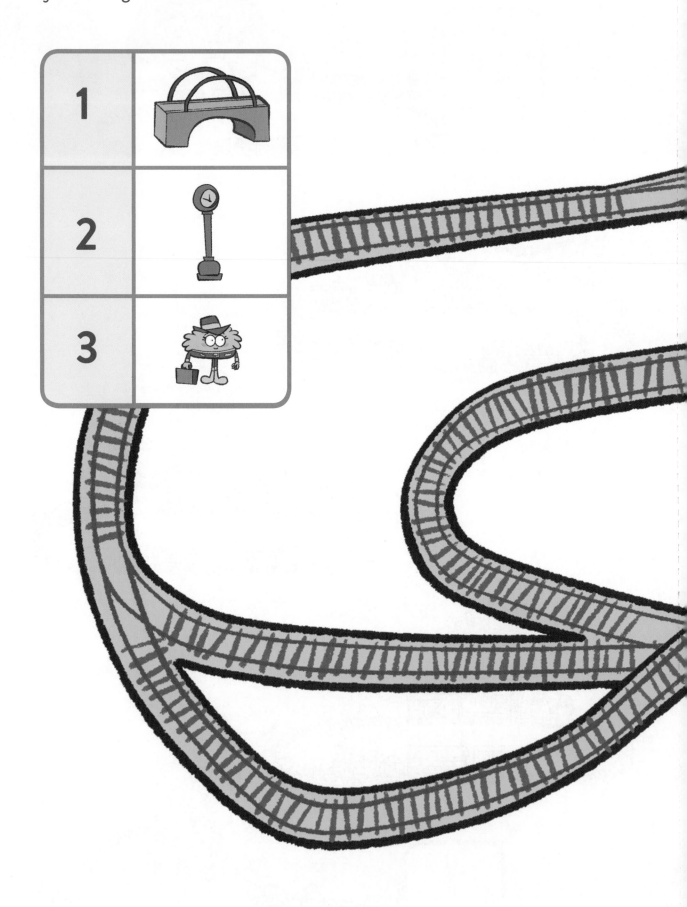

LET'S START!

GATHER THESE TOOLS AND MATERIALS.

 Crayons or markers

 3 or more shoebox lids

 Scissors (with an adult's help)

 Tape

 Shoebox

 Toilet paper tube

Construction paper

 Glue or glue stick

 Small toys

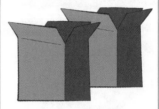 Cardboard boxes

 Chairs

LET'S TINKER!

Gather your materials. How many of each type of object do you have? **Arrange** each group in different ways—scattered, in a circle, or in a line. What happens to the number of objects? Does the number change or stay the same when the objects are arranged differently?

LET'S MAKE: LOCOMOTIVE ENGINE!

1. With the help of an adult, **cut** 1 shoebox lid in half widthwise.

2. With the help of an adult, **cut** a window in each half lid.

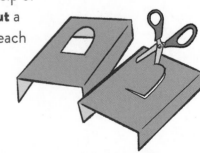

3. Tape the flat side of the lids to the box.

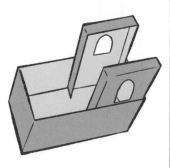

4. With the help of an adult, **cut** the sides off the remaining shoebox lids.

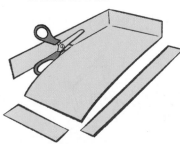

5. Bend the lids slightly so they are curved. Then **tape** them to the shoebox.

6. Tape the toilet paper tube on the front for the smokestack.

7. Decorate your locomotive and put your toys in for a ride!

LET'S ENGINEER!

The MotMots in Tinker Town would like to visit their penpals in Bungleburg, but there is a canyon between the two towns.

How can the MotMots visit their friends?

Put two chairs a small distance apart to act as your cliffs. The ground in between is the bottom of your canyon! Then **build** a bridge between them using your materials. **Make** the bridge large enough for your shoebox train to cross. Then **test** it out! Will the bridge hold your train? **Put** some items in your train. **Count** them aloud as you place them inside. How many items can you add before your bridge breaks?

PROJECT 7: DONE!
Get your sticker!

Addition Up to 5

Count how many toys are in each row. Say the number aloud. Next, draw one more toy in each row. How many toys are there now? Write the number.

Count how many toys are in each column. Say the number aloud. Then follow the directions.

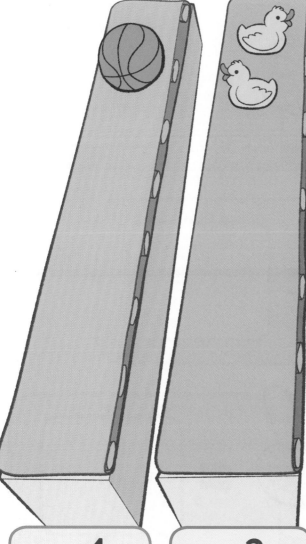

Draw **4** more balls. Count the balls again. How many balls are there now? Write the number.

Draw **3** more ducks. Count the ducks again. How many ducks are there now? Write the number.

Draw **2** more drums. Count the drums again. How many drums are there now? Write the number.

Draw **1** more top. Count the tops again. How many tops are there now? Write the number.

Count how many fingers are showing on each hand below. How many fingers are there in all? Say the number aloud and write the number.

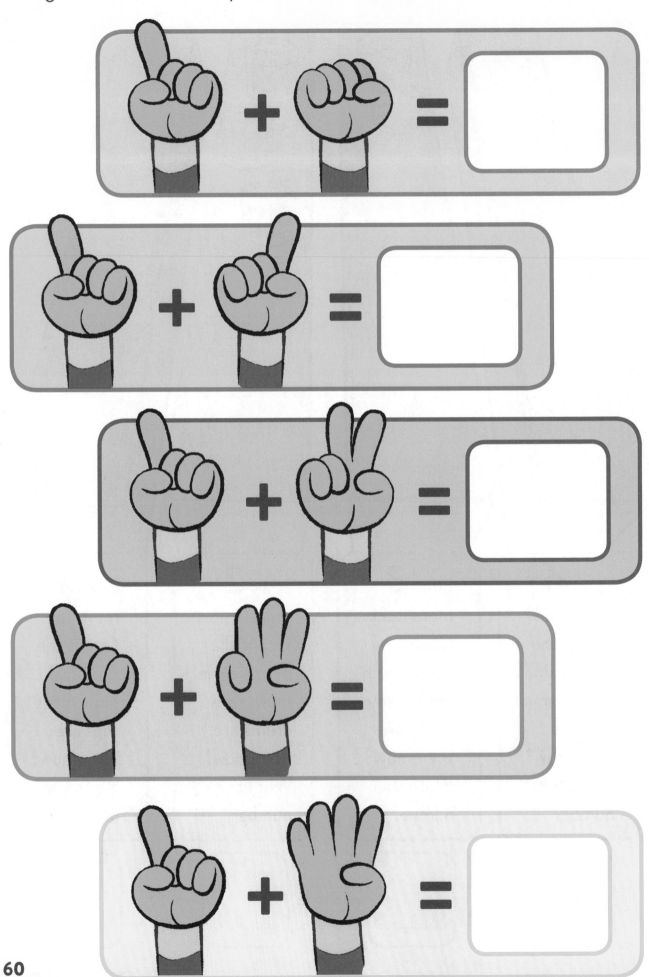

Use your own hands to add! Copy the MotMot hands and count your own fingers. How many fingers are there in all?

Read about the toys each MotMot is making. Then answer each question.

Enid paints 1 train. Then she paints 2 more. How many trains does she paint in all?

1 + 2 = _____

Brian folds 2 paper airplanes. Then he folds 1 more. How many airplanes does he fold in all?

2 + 1 = _____

Frank makes 3 dolls. Then he makes 2 more. How many dolls does he make in all?

3 + 2 = _____

Dimitri makes 2 kites. Then he makes 3 more. How many kites does he make in all?

2 + 3 = _____

Count how many toys are in each group. Then count how many toys there are in all. Last, write the numbers and, with the help of an adult, read the number sentences aloud.

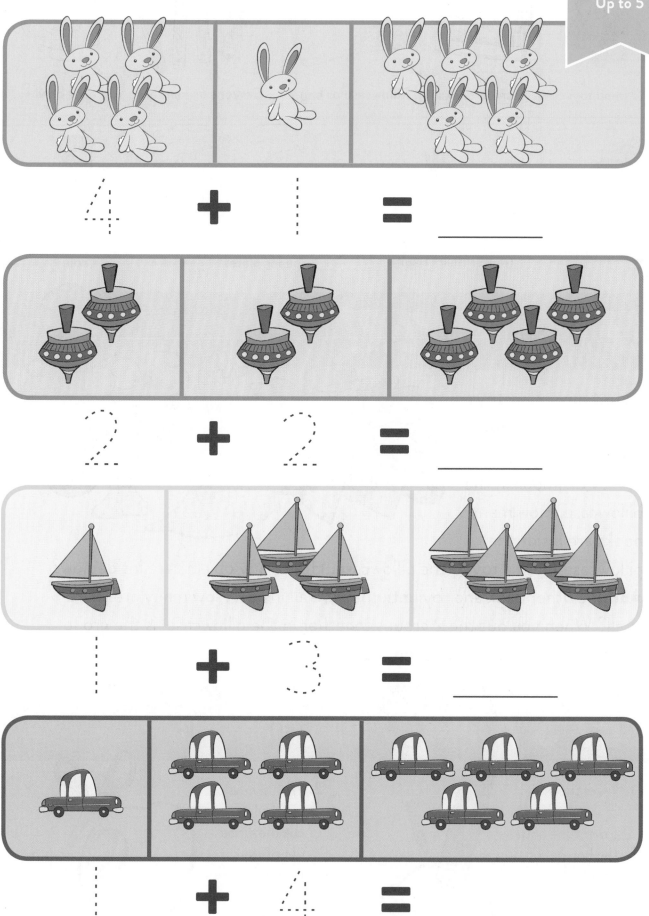

63

LET'S START!

GATHER THESE TOOLS AND MATERIALS.

 2 small toys

 2 small books

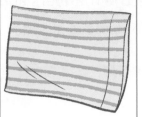 Pillowcase or bag

 Crayons or markers

 Paper bowl

 Paper towel roll

 Scissors (with an adult's help)

6 or more paper plates

Toilet paper roll

LET'S TINKER!

Count how many toys you have. Now, **count** how many books you have. **Put** 1 book in the pillowcase. How many books are inside the pillowcase? **Add** a toy to the pillowcase. How many objects are inside now? **Add** the other book and toy until they are all inside. How many are there in all? When you put the 2 groups together in the pillowcase, is the group bigger or smaller than when they were separate?

LET'S MAKE: RING TOSS TOY!

1. **Trace** the end of the paper towel tube onto the bottom of a paper bowl.

2. With the help of an adult, **cut** the circle out of the bowl to create a hole.

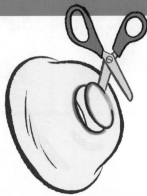

3. Fit the paper towel tube into the hole to make a stake.

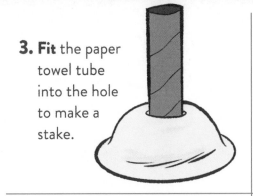

4. With the help of an adult, **cut** the center out of 6 paper plates to make your rings.

5. Color and decorate 3 rings one way. Then **color** and decorate. 3 rings another way.

6. Find a partner and play! Each player chooses their own ring color, and then takes turns, throwing one ring at a time until all of them have been thrown. **Score** 2 points for each ringer and 1 point for any ring touching the stake. **Pick up** the rings and continue playing until one player reaches 5 points.

LET'S ENGINEER!

Frank and Brian were playing ring toss, but the game was too hard! Neither MotMot could get their rings around the stake.

How can the MotMots make the game easier?

Make your ring toss toy easier. **Try** bringing the stake closer, adding more rings so each player gets more tries, making a shorter stake, or changing the rules of the game completely! What other ways can you make it easier? Once you think of a new way to play, **ask** another person to play. At the end of each game, **count** each person's points to find out who won. You can also **add** your points together. How many points do you have in all? Can you break your record? **Play** again!

PROJECT 8: DONE!
Get your sticker!

Subtraction Under 5

How many balloons does each MotMot have? Count them aloud, then cross out 1 balloon in each group to pop it. How many balloons are left? Count the remaining balloons and write the number.

How many white balloons does each MotMot have? Count them aloud, then color 1 balloon in each group. How many white balloons are left? Write the number.

The MotMots are playing Enid Says Subtract. Read the prompt aloud and use your fingers to subtract. Then write the number.

ENID SAYS SUBTRACT 1 FROM 5.

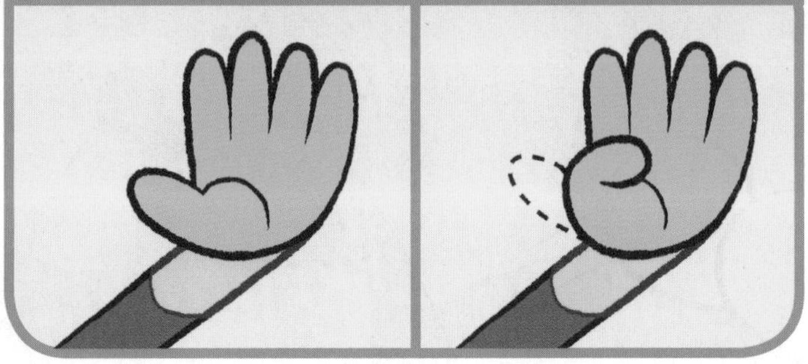

5 – 1 = 4

ENID SAYS SUBTRACT 2 FROM 5.

5 – 2 = ___

ENID SAYS SUBTRACT 2 FROM 3.

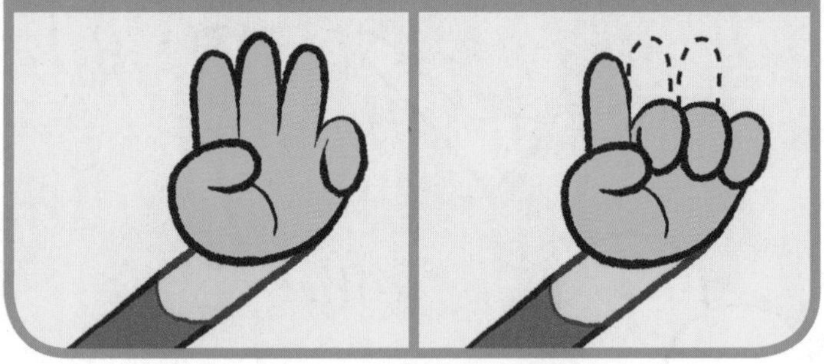

3 – 2 = ___

ENID SAYS SUBTRACT 1 FROM 4.

4 – 1 = _____

ENID SAYS SUBTRACT 4 FROM 5.

5 – 4 = _____

ENID SAYS SUBTRACT 3 FROM 5.

5 – 3 = _____

How many fingers should be up to begin? How many fingers should you put down? The number of fingers that are left up is your answer!

Read about the food each MotMot ate at Tinker Town's annual barbecue. Then write the answer to each question.

There were **5** hot dogs. Frank ate **2**. How many hot dogs were left?

  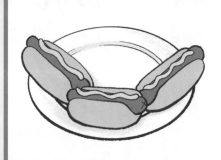

5   –   2   = ___

There were **3** hamburgers. Enid ate **2**. How many hamburgers were left?

3   –   2   = ___

There was **1** cup of lemonade. Brian drank it. How many cups of lemonade were left?

1   –   1   = ___

Count the food on each plate aloud. Then trace the missing numbers. Last, say aloud and write how much food was left over.

3 − 1 = _____

4 − 2 = _____

2 − 1 = _____

5 − 4 = _____

LET'S START! GATHER THESE TOOLS AND MATERIALS.

5 crayons or markers

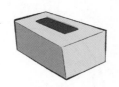
Empty rectangular tissue box

Green paint or green construction paper

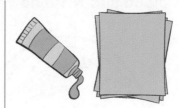
Scissors (with an adult's help)

White construction paper

Glue or glue stick

Up to 5 small snacks such as popcorn, nuts, mini pretzels, etc.

Cardboard boxes

Tape

LET'S TINKER!

Play Hide-and-Seek Subtraction! **Get** a partner and count how many crayons or markers you have. Now **ask** your partner to hide one. How many are left? **Find** the missing object and put it back with the rest. How many do you have in all? **Play** again by hiding 2, 3, 4, or all 5 crayons or markers.

LET'S MAKE: HUNGRY AMELIA!

1. **Paint** your tissue box green or cover it with green construction paper. **Let** dry.

2. With the help of an adult, **cut** the edge of the white construction paper for Amelia's teeth. Then **draw** and cut Amelia's eyeballs and cheeks.

3. **Glue** the teeth to the bottom of the tissue box right inside the opening.

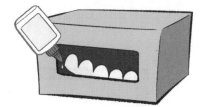

4. **Glue** Amelia's eyeballs and rosy cheeks.

5. **Feed** Amelia! **Count** how many snacks you have. Then **feed** Amelia 1 snack. How many snacks are left? **Keep feeding** Amelia 1 snack at a time and count how many are left. Can you feed her all the snacks so there are none left?

LET'S ENGINEER!

Every year Frank makes 4 apple pies for the Tinker Town barbecue. And every year, 2 pies go missing!

How can Frank protect his pies?

Draw 4 apple pies on paper and, with the help of an adult, cut them out. If 2 pies go missing, how many are left? **Build** something to protect your remaining pies!

PROJECT 9: DONE!
Get your sticker!

Comparing Quantities

Count how many objects are in each cubby. Then circle the group that has **more** in each row.

Count how many objects are in each cubby. Then circle the group that has **less** in each row.

Draw lines to pair the objects. Are there **more**, **less**, or the **same** number of each group of objects? Finish each sentence by circling the correct answer.

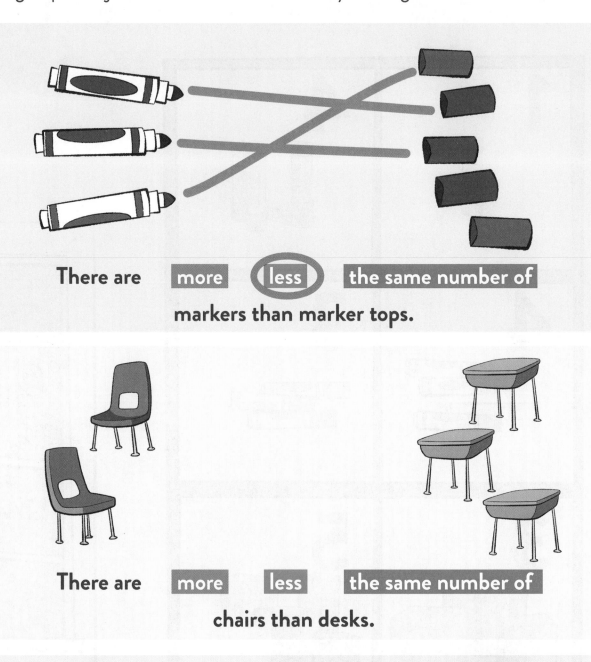

There are | more | (less) | the same number of
markers than marker tops.

There are | more | less | the same number of
chairs than desks.

There are | more | less | the same number of
books as backpacks.

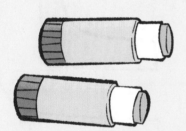

There are   **more**   **less**   **the same number of**
sandwiches than lunch boxes.

There are   **more**   **less**   **the same number of**
glue sticks as glue tops.

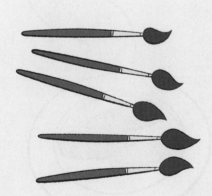

There are   **more**   **less**   **the same number of**
paintbrushes than paint bottles.

Count how many snacks each MotMot has aloud. Draw lines through the maze so each MotMot gets more of his or her snack.

Now how many snacks does each MotMot have in all? Say it aloud.

Add stickers from page 385 so each pair of MotMots has the same number of snacks.

LET'S START!

GATHER THESE TOOLS AND MATERIALS.

1 to 5 paper cups

1 to 5 drinking straws

Pillowcase

Paper plate

Scissors (with an adult's help)

Crayons

Brad

Paper clips

Small snacks, like nuts, popcorn, baby carrots, etc.

4 toilet paper rolls

Small piece of cardboard or cereal box

Stuffed animal

LET'S TINKER!

Count how many paper cups and straws you have. Do you have more of one or the other? Or do you have the same number of cups and straws? Now, **test** it out! **Gather** your paper cups and straws in the pillowcase and shake it up. **Pull** 1 item out at a time and match each cup with a straw. **Keep matching** until your pillowcase is empty. Does every cup have a matching straw?

LET'S MAKE: SPINNING SNACKS!

1. With the help of an adult, **poke** a small hole in the center of the paper plate using scissors.

2. **Draw** 3 lines from the center of the paper plate, like so:

3. In different sections **write** "More," "Less," or "Same," like so:

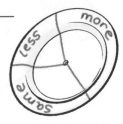

4. **Poke** a brad through the hole in the paper plate. **Bend** the back side of the brad so the paper plate can move and so a paper clip can fit.

5. **Attach** the paper clip to the brad. It should spin freely.

6. **Get** a friend or family member and play Spinning Snacks! **Choose** a snack as the prize. Then **spin** the paper clip. **Read** the word where the paper clip stops. If you **land** on "More" then you can take more snacks than the other player. If you **land** on "Less," take less, and if you land on "Same," share the snacks equally. Next, it's your partner's turn to **pick** a snack and spin!

LET'S ENGINEER!

Dimitri wants to have snack time with his 3 favorite stuffed bears—but he only has enough stools for himself and 2 of the bears.

How can Dimitri sit with all the bears?

Build a stool for your own stuffed animal. Once your stuffed animal can sit, **share** some snacks. **Count out** the snacks so everyone gets the same amount. Then enjoy your snacks together!

PROJECT 10: DONE!
Get your sticker!

Circle the object that is **bigger** in each row. Then underline the object that is **smaller**.

Circle the object that is **taller** in each scene. Then underline the object that is **shorter**.

Circle the object that is **longer** in each row. Then underline the object that is **shorter**.

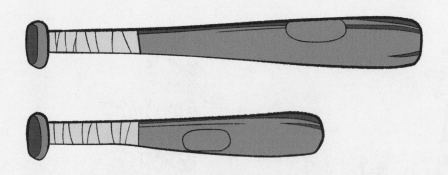

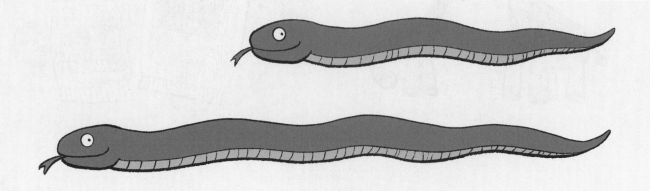

Circle the object that is **heavier** in each box. Then underline the object that is **lighter**.

Circle the **tallest** MotMot in each row. Underline the **shortest** MotMot in each row.

AMELIA   BRIAN   FRANK

DIMITRI   ENID   CALLIE

With the help of an adult, cut out the MotMots on page 86. Then place each MotMot next to the ride entrance. Which MotMots can ride on the roller coaster? Say their names aloud.

You must be

THIS ▶
TALL

to ride

LET'S START!

GATHER THESE TOOLS AND MATERIALS.

Toys of various sizes, such as vehicles, instruments, blocks, etc.

Scissors (with an adult's help)

Optional: hole puncher

2 paper cups

2 pieces of string (about 12 inches long)

Plastic hanger with hooks or notches

3 strings of various lengths

Tape

LET'S TINKER!

Arrange your toys by size—from biggest to smallest, or smallest to biggest. What if you arrange the toys only by height? Will your arrangement change? Why or why not? **Try** arranging by length and weight, too. How many other ways can you arrange your toys?

LET'S MAKE: TOY SCALE!

1. With the help of an adult, **use** your hole puncher or scissors to punch a hole through both sides of a paper cup.

2. With the help of an adult, **tie** the ends of a 12-inch piece of string to the holes in the cup.

3. **Repeat** steps 1 and 2 with the other cup and 12-inch string—these are the buckets for your scale!

---

4. **Place** the string into the notches or hooks of the hanger so the cups hang down.

5. **Place** the hanger where it can swing easily, like on a shower rod or drying rack.

---

6. **Weigh** your toys! **Put** a different toy in each bucket. Which bucket hangs lower than the other? Which toy weighs more? **Compare** all your toys.

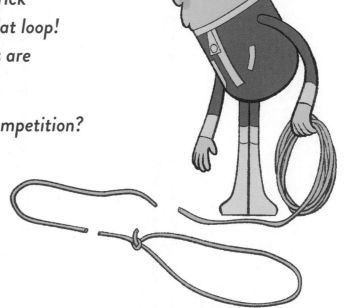

LET'S ENGINEER!

Dimitri wants to enter the lasso trick competition—he can do a great flat loop! But his lasso broke and the pieces are too short to finish the trick!

How can Dimitri still enter the competition?

Look at your remaining pieces of string. How can you make them longer? Can you put them back together somehow?

PROJECT 11: DONE!
Get your sticker!

Units of Measurement

Look at each crane. Then draw buildings that are as **tall** as each crane.

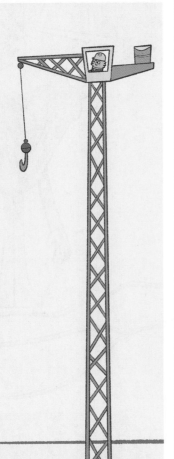

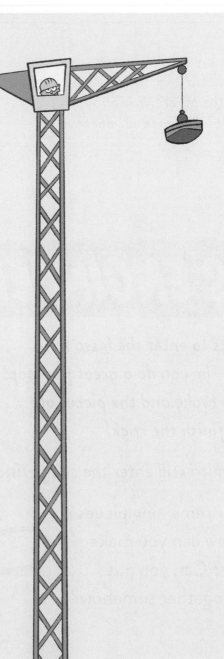

Look at each pipe. Then draw metal beams that are as **long** as each pipe.

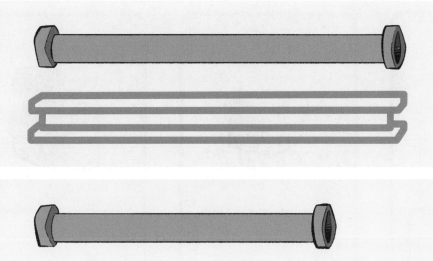

How **tall** is each stack of bricks? Count aloud how many bricks are in each stack. Then write the number.

How **long** is each track of carts? Count aloud how many carts are on each track. Then write the number.

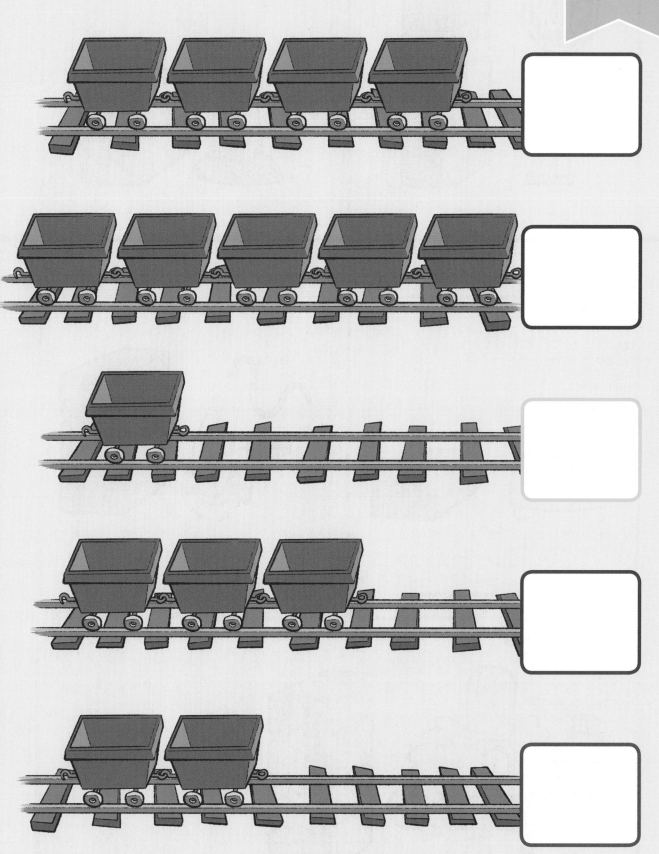

How many bricks **tall** is each object? Count how many bricks are beside each object. Then write the number.

How many bricks **long** is each object? Count how many bricks are underneath each object. Then write the number.

_____

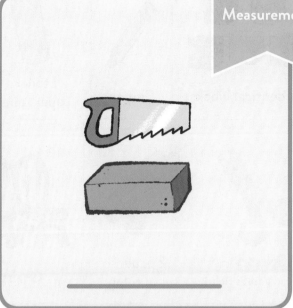

_____

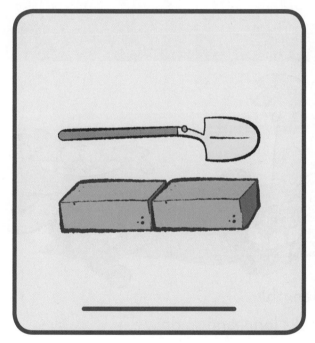

_____

_____

_____

LET'S START! GATHER THESE TOOLS AND MATERIALS.

5 identical blocks	Crayon	1 toilet paper tube	String	Tape	Construction paper

Scissors (with an adult's help)	2 paper towel tubes	Chairs	Sheets		Pillows or sofa cushions

LET'S TINKER!

Go on a measurement hunt! **Find** objects that are 1 block tall, 2 blocks tall, 3 blocks tall, 4 blocks tall, and 5 blocks tall. If you can't find an object that is the correct height, **draw** one or make your own. Then **do** the same for length! **Find** objects that are 1 block long, 2 blocks long, and so on.

LET'S MAKE: PAPER CRANE!

1. With the help of an adult, **cut** a toilet paper tube in half widthwise.

2. **Run** the string through the tube and tape it in place. This is your basket!

3. With the help of an adult, **draw** and cut a triangle out of construction paper to make the top of your crane.

4. Tape the string of your basket to an end of the triangle.

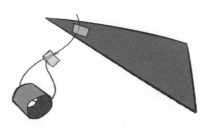

5. With the help of an adult, **make** two cuts across from each other on one end of the paper towel roll.

6. Insert the top of your crane in the cuts and stand your crane up. Can your crane hold any of your materials?

LET'S ENGINEER!

The tunnel in Tinker Town's park collapsed! The MotMots have to build a new tunnel. But first, they need to know how tall to make it so that MotMots can walk through.

How can the MotMots find out how tall to make the new tunnel?

Plan and build a tunnel that you can walk through using pillows, sheets, and chairs. How tall must your tunnel be? What can you use to measure the height of your body? How can you make sure the sides of your tunnel are the right height?

PROJECT 12: DONE!
Get your sticker!

Spatial Reasoning

Color the books on the top shelf **red**. Then color the books on the bottom shelf **blue**.

Circle the MotMots that are **in front** of the bookshelves.
Underline the MotMots that are **next to** the bookshelves.

Find the MotMots that are **behind**
the bookshelves. How many are
there? Say the number aloud.

Circle the MotMots that are walking **up** the stairs. Underline the MotMots that are walking **down** the stairs.

MATH BOOKS

SCIENCE BOOKS

HISTORY BOOKS

PICTURE BOOKS

Get the MotMot stickers from page 385. Place the MotMots **on** the carpet for story time!

Find the MotMots **in** the reading nooks.
How many are there? Say the number aloud.

If you wrote a book, what would you write about? First, draw a picture of what you would like to write about. Then write 1 word about your book **above** your picture. Last, write your name **under** your picture.

My Book About

_____

by _____

Circle the MotMot that is **first** in each line. Then underline the MotMot that is **last** in each line.

LET'S START!

GATHER THESE TOOLS AND MATERIALS.

Large cardboard box

10 craft sticks

Tape

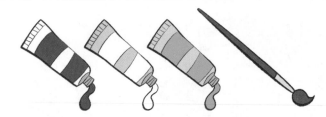

Paint and paintbrush

Scissors
(with an adult's help)

LET'S TINKER!

Get your cardboard box and act out each location: go **in front of** your box, go **behind** it, go **next to** it, and then go **inside** it. Is it still a box each time? Maybe it's a cave once you're inside it! Maybe it's the counter of an ice cream shop when you're next to it! What other ways can you move around your box?

LET'S MAKE: YOUR PERSONAL PUZZLE!

1. **Place** your craft sticks side by side and tape them together with 2 or 3 pieces of tape.

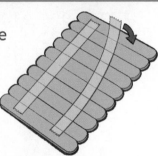

2. Flip the sticks over so the tape is on the bottom, and paint a picture on them. This will be your puzzle.

3. Wait for the paint to dry. Then **remove** the tape.

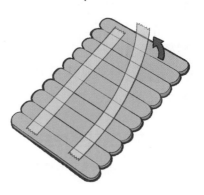

4. Move and mix up your puzzle parts! Can you put your painting back together? Which craft stick is first? Which is last? Which ones are in the middle?

LET'S ENGINEER!

Brian wants to go to the library, but he has to put his shoes on first. The problem is, he can't remember which is his left shoe and which is his right shoe!

How can Brian remember which shoe goes on which foot?

Get a pair of your own shoes. How do you tell which is the shoe for your left foot and which is for your right foot? **Use** your materials and the stickers on page 385 to help you know which shoe goes on which foot.

PROJECT 13: DONE!
Get your sticker!

2D Shapes

A **square** ■ is a flat shape with 4 sides that are the same length, as well as 4 corners.

A **rectangle** ▬ is a flat shape with 2 longer sides and 2 shorter sides, as well as 4 corners.

Use your finger to trace the **rectangles** and **squares** in each painting. Count the number of sides aloud as you trace.

Draw your own rectangle or square on the blank canvas. Count the number of sides aloud as you draw. Then color in your art!

Find the rectangles and squares in the painting
and sculpture. Then color in the shapes.

How many sides does a rectangle have?

How many sides does a square have?

A **triangle** 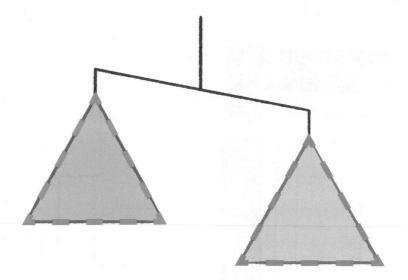 is a flat shape with 3 sides.

Trace the **triangles** on the mobile. Count the number of sides aloud as you trace.

Draw your own triangles on the empty mobile. Count the number of sides aloud as you draw. Then color your triangle art!

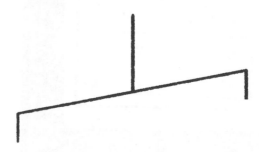

How many sides does a triangle have?

Circle each piece of art that has a triangle in it.

A **circle**  is a flat shape made by a curved line. It has no sides.

Trace each **circle**. Describe the shape aloud as you trace.

How many sides does a circle have?

Draw and color your own
circle on the empty pedestal!

Draw lines to match the objects to their shapes. Then say the shapes aloud.

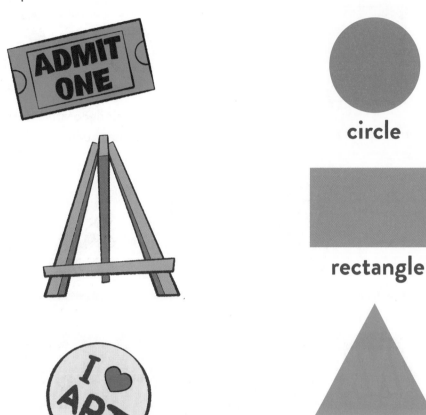

circle

rectangle

triangle

Find objects around you that are shaped like rectangles, squares, circles, and triangles. Then draw them below.

LET'S START! GATHER THESE TOOLS AND MATERIALS.

Scissors (with an adult's help)

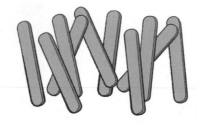

Construction paper

Glue stick

Optional: decorative items such as ribbon, beads, feathers, etc.

White paper

10 or more craft sticks

Crayons or markers

LET'S TINKER!

With the help of an adult, **cut out** the rectangles and squares on page 106, the triangles on page 108, and the circles on page 110. **Flip** them, turn them around, and look at their size. Do the shapes remain the same? Now, **close** your eyes, pick up one shape, and feel the edges of the paper. **Count** the number of sides and name the shape.

LET'S MAKE: 2D SHAPE COLLAGE!

1. **Arrange** the shapes you cut out from pages 106, 108, and 110 onto a sheet of paper. (If you need more shapes, **fold**, tear, or cut more out of construction paper with the help of an adult.)

2. Once you have an arrangement you like, **glue** each shape onto the paper.

3. You can **add** materials like ribbon, beads, feathers, or other objects to decorate your collage.

LET'S ENGINEER!

Tinker Town's art museum is opening a gallery called Shape Space! Amelia wants to make some new shape art for the gallery, but she only has craft sticks.

How can Amelia make different shapes using only her craft sticks?

Use your craft sticks to make different shapes on a white piece of paper. How can you combine the craft sticks to make a shape? What shapes can you make? Are there any shapes you can't make with craft sticks? Why or why not? Once you are done arranging your shapes, **glue** them to the paper and decorate your piece of art.

PROJECT 14: DONE!
Get your sticker!

Combining 2D Shapes

Draw a line to complete each shape. Then name each shape aloud.

TINKER
TOWN

NATURE PATH

Look at the key, and finish the picture by filling in each shape with the correct color.

COLOR KEY
Square:
Triangle:
Circle:
Rectangle:

Look at the key. Finish the picture by filling in each shape with the color that matches its features.

COLOR KEY

A shape that has 3 sides: **green**

A shape that has
no straight sides: **yellow**

A shape that has 4 sides that are
all the same length: **brown**

Draw a line to match each pair of shapes to their combined shape.

With the help of an adult, cut out the shapes on page 118 and rearrange them into your own forest scene. Then glue them onto this page, and draw any other shapes you may need to finish the scene.

LET'S START!

Blocks of different shapes

Crayons or markers

Construction paper

Plastic bin or bucket

Rice, beans, or cornmeal

Scissors
(with an adult's help)

Glue

Tape

LET'S TINKER!

Trace the outline of your blocks onto a piece of construction paper. Then **fill** your bin with rice, beans, or cornmeal. **Bury** your blocks inside so you can't see them anymore. **Reach** into the bin and feel a block. Before pulling it out, **say** what shape it will match on the paper. Then **pull** out the block and put it on the paper to see if you are right. **Continue** matching blocks until there are no more shapes left.

LET'S MAKE: CIRCLE AND SQUARE BIRDS!

1. With the help of an adult, **cut** out a circle and a square from construction paper for the bird bodies.

2. **Glue** these shapes to a piece of white or light-colored construction paper.

3. With the help of an adult, **cut** out 6 small triangles for the beaks and feet. Then **glue** 3 of the triangles to each body.

4. With the help of an adult, **cut** out 2 white circles and 2 smaller black circles for the eyes. **Glue** each white circle onto a body, and each black circle onto a white circle.

5. With the help of an adult, **cut** out 4 half circles for the wings and hair. Then **glue** each set to a body.

6. Display your bird art somewhere special!

LET'S ENGINEER!

The bees in Bungleburg need a new home—and fast! A bear escaped from the zoo and knocked down all the bees' hives and ate all their honey. The MotMots want to help, but they don't have many materials—just paper and a few tools.

How can the MotMots make a new home for the bees with their materials?

Build the inside of a beehive using paper and your other tools. What shape can you make with paper that looks close to the hive cells that bees climb into? How can you make a lot of those shapes and connect them so many bees can live together?

PROJECT 15: DONE!
Get your sticker!

ANSWER KEY

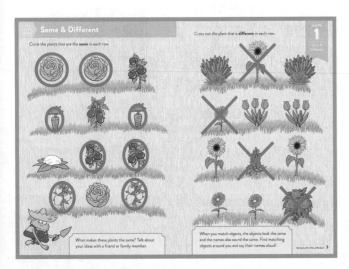

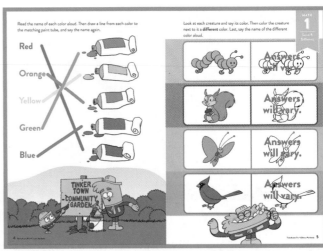

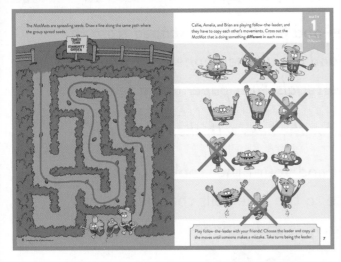

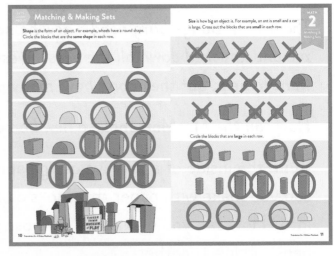

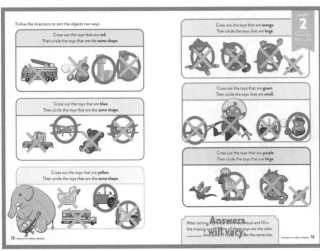

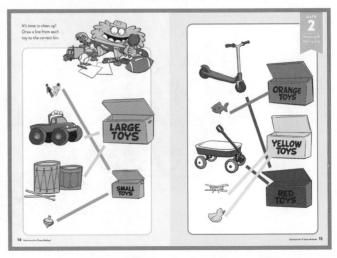

Counting to 10

Follow the path from 1 to 5 with your finger and say each number aloud. Then draw a line from 1 to 5 to complete the picture.

RING TOSS

Tinker Town Street Fair

Count how many fingers each MotMot is holding up. Then trace the number.

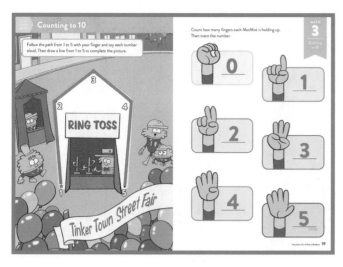

0
1
2
3
4
5

Follow the path from 0 to 10 with your finger and say each number aloud. Then draw a line from 0 to 10 to complete the picture.

BALLOON ANIMALS by AMELIA

Count how many fingers each MotMot is holding up. Then trace the number.

6
7
8
9
10

The MotMots are playing Enid Says Count Aloud! Play along with them by following each direction and counting aloud.

ENID SAYS

Enid Says: Touch your nose **5** times.

Enid Says: Touch your toes **3** times.

Enid Says: Jump **8** times.

Enid Says: Stomp your feet **10** times.

Play your own game of Enid Says Count Aloud! Get some friends and choose a leader. The leader says what the other players must do and how many times they must do it. But only follow commands that begin with the words "Enid Says." Listen carefully! If you do an action without the leader saying "Enid Says," you're out!

Look at the key, and color the MotMots by matching each number to a color.

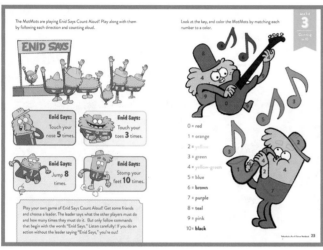

0 = red
1 = orange
2 = yellow
3 = green
4 = yellow-green
5 = blue
6 = brown
7 = purple
8 = teal
9 = pink
10 = black

Quantities 0–5 & Writing 0–5

Count how many pieces of fruit are in each basket. Then write the total number in each basket.

1
2
3
4
5

Hint! You can cross out each piece of fruit as you count so you don't count anything twice.

Count how many of each kind of vegetable are in the basket. Then write the total numbers of each kind of vegetable.

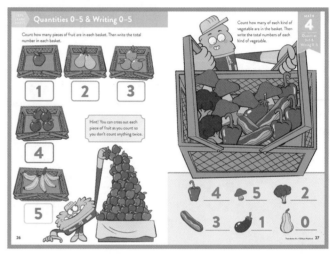

4
5
2
3
1
0

Count aloud how many items are in each checkout aisle. The last number you say is the number of objects in the group! Write the total number of items.

2
4
3
5
0

Read the poems aloud to count each group. Then write the number of items in the group.

I count **1** and **2**.
I count **2** stews.

I count **1, 2,** and **3**.
I count **3** bags of frozen peas.

I count **1, 2, 3,** and **4**.
I count **4** pears in the store.

I count **1** cinnamon bun.
Counting food is a lot of fun!

Answers will vary.

With the help of an adult, cut out the items below the baskets. Then sort them into groups. How many of each item do you have? Match the number of items to the correct basket by placing the items on top.

1
2
3
4
5

The MotMots are buying food for a party! Count the number of items each MotMot wants to buy. Then write the number on the cart.

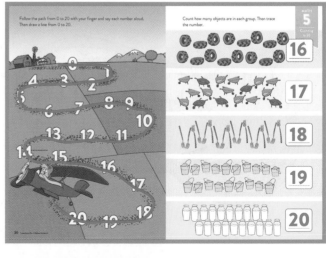

1
2
5
4

Counting to 20

Follow the path from 0 to 15 with your finger and say each number aloud. Then draw a line from 0 to 15.

Count aloud how many animals or objects are in each group. Then trace the number.

11 pigs
12 hens
13 eggs
14 mice
15 chicks

Follow the path from 0 to 20 with your finger and say each number aloud. Then draw a line from 0 to 20.

Count how many objects are in each group. Then trace the number.

16
17
18
19
20

Enid loves eating beans. She loves them so much that she planted 19 different bean plants! Follow the path from 0 to 19 with your finger. Then draw a line from 0 to 19 to connect the bean plants.

0 1 2 3 4 5
10 9 8 7 6
11 12 13 14 15 16
19 18 17

If Enid planted 1 more bean plant, how many plants would she have?

Color in the correct number of stalls.

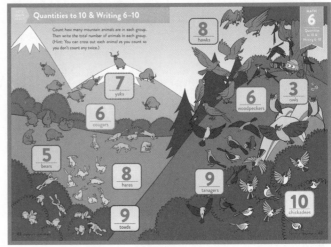

Count how many mountain animals are in each group. Then write the total number of animals in each group. (Hint: You can cross out each animal as you count so you don't count any twice.)

8 hawks
7 yaks
6 cougars
6 woodpeckers
3 owls
5 bears
8 hares
9 toads
9 tanagers
10 chickadees

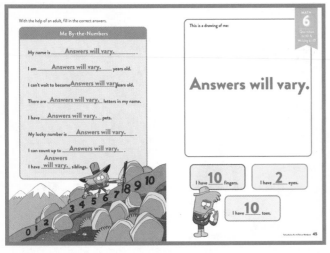

With the help of an adult, fill in the correct answers.

Me By-the-Numbers

My name is Answers will vary.
I am Answers will vary. years old.
I can't wait to become Answers will vary. years old.
There are Answers will vary. letters in my name.
I have Answers will vary. pets.
My lucky number is Answers will vary.
I can count up to Answers will vary.
I have Answers will vary. siblings.

This is a drawing of me:

Answers will vary.

I have 10 fingers. I have 2 eyes.
I have 10 toes.

Frank is having a picnic for his friends! Read Frank's menu and use the stickers from page 385 to add the correct amount of food for the picnic.

6 10 7

Draw a line through the maze so that each MetMot collects the correct number of objects on their hike.

Dimitri wants to collect 9 leaves.
Callie wants to collect 8 acorns.
Enid wants to collect 10 sticks.

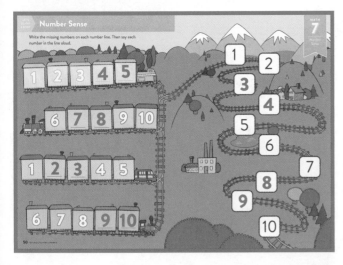

Number Sense

Write the missing numbers on each number line. Then say each number in the line aloud.

1 2 3 4 5
6 7 8 9 10
1 2 3 4 5
6 7 8 9 10

1 2 3 4 5 6 7 8 9 10

Complete the picture by drawing a line from each starting number ★ to 10. Say each number aloud as you go.

Count how many trains are in each group. Then write the number.

3 5 5 2 2

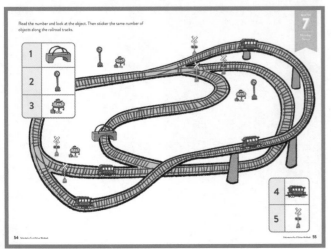

Read the number and look at the object. Then sticker the same number of objects along the railroad tracks.

1 2 3
4 5

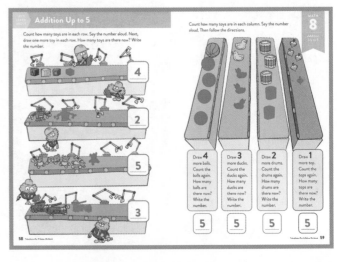

Addition Up to 5

Count how many toys are in each row. Say the number aloud. Next, draw one more toy in each row. How many toys are there now? Write the number.

4 2 5 3

Count how many toys are in each column. Say the number aloud. Then follow the directions.

Draw 4 more balls. Count the balls again. How many balls are there now? Write the number.

Draw 3 more ducks. Count the ducks again. How many ducks are there now? Write the number.

Draw 2 more drums. Count the drums again. How many drums are there now? Write the number.

Draw 1 more top. Count the tops again. How many tops are there now? Write the number.

5 5 5 5

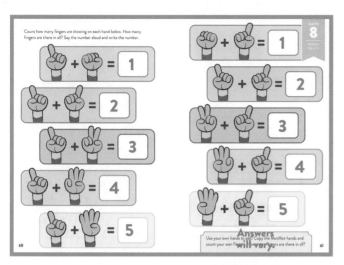

Count how many fingers are showing on each hand below. How many fingers are there in all? Say the number aloud and write the number.

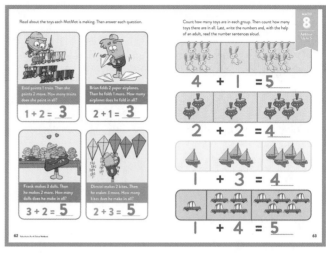

Use your own hands to add! Copy the MotMot hands and count your own fingers. How many fingers are there in all?

Answers will vary

Read about the toys each MotMot is making. Then answer each question.

Enid points 1 train. Then she paints 2 more. How many trains does she paint in all?
1 + 2 = 3

Brian folds 2 paper airplanes. Then he folds 1 more. How many airplanes does he fold in all?
2 + 1 = 3

Frank makes 3 dolls. Then he makes 2 more. How many dolls does he make in all?
3 + 2 = 5

Dimitri makes 2 kites. Then he makes 3 more. How many kites does he make in all?
2 + 3 = 5

Count how many toys are in each group. Then count how many toys there are in all. Last, write the numbers and, with the help of an adult, read the number sentences aloud.

4 + 1 = 5
2 + 2 = 4
1 + 3 = 4
1 + 4 = 5

Subtraction Under 5

How many balloons does each MotMot have? Count them aloud, then cross out 1 balloon in each group to pop it. How many balloons are left? Count the remaining balloons and write the number.

How many white balloons does each MotMot have? Count them aloud, then color 1 balloon in each group. How many white balloons are left? Write the number.

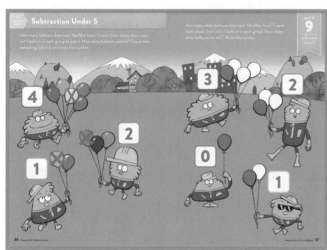

The MotMots are playing Enid Says Subtract. Read the prompt aloud and use your fingers to subtract. Then write the number.

ENID SAYS SUBTRACT 1 FROM 5.
5 – 1 = 4

ENID SAYS SUBTRACT 2 FROM 5.
5 – 2 = 3

ENID SAYS SUBTRACT 2 FROM 3.
3 – 2 = 1

ENID SAYS SUBTRACT 1 FROM 4.
4 – 1 = 3

ENID SAYS SUBTRACT 4 FROM 5.
5 – 4 = 1

ENID SAYS SUBTRACT 3 FROM 5.
5 – 3 = 2

How many fingers should be up to begin? How many fingers should you put down? The number of fingers that are left up is your answer!

Read about the food each MotMot ate at Tinker Town's annual barbecue. Then write the answer to each question.

There were 5 hot dogs. Frank ate 2. How many hot dogs were left?
5 – 2 = 3

There were 3 hamburgers. Enid ate 2. How many hamburgers were left?
3 – 2 = 1

There was 1 cup of lemonade. Brian drank it. How many cups of lemonade were left?
1 – 1 = 0

Count the food on each plate aloud. Then trace the missing numbers. Last, say aloud and write how much food was left over.

3 – 1 = 2
4 – 2 = 2
2 – 1 = 1
5 – 4 = 1

Comparing Quantities

Count how many objects are in each cubby. Then circle the group that has more in each row.

Count how many objects are in each cubby. Then circle the group that has less in each row.

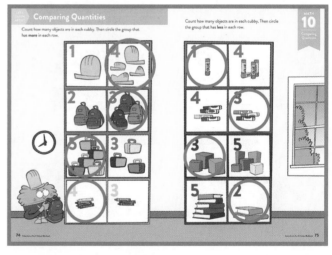

Draw lines to pair the objects. Are there more, less, or the same number of each group of objects? Finish each sentence by circling the correct answer.

There are more / less / the same number of markers than marker tops.

There are more / less / the same number of chairs than desks.

There are more / less / the same number of books as backpacks.

There are more / less / the same number of sandwiches than lunch boxes.

There are more / less / the same number of glue sticks as glue tops.

There are more / less / the same number of paintbrushes than paint bottles.

Count how many snacks each MotMot has aloud. Draw lines through the maze so each MotMot gets more of his or her snack.

Answers will vary!

Now how many snacks does each MotMot have in all? Say it aloud.

Add stickers from page 385 so each pair of MotMots has the same number of snacks.

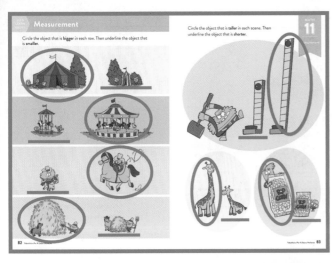

Measurement

Circle the object that is **bigger** in each row. Then underline the object that is **smaller**.

Circle the object that is **taller** in each scene. Then underline the object that is **shorter**.

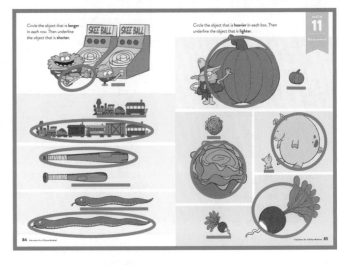

Circle the object that is **longer** in each row. Then underline the object that is **shorter**.

Circle the object that is **heavier** in each box. Then underline the object that is **lighter**.

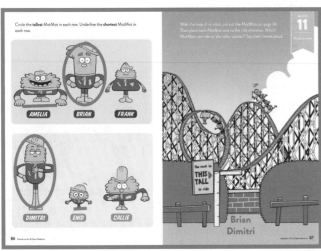

Circle the **tallest** MotMot in each row. Underline the **shortest** MotMot in each row.

AMELIA   BRIAN   FRANK

DIMITRI   ENID   CALLIE

With the help of an adult, cut out the MotMots on page 369. Then place each MotMot next to the ride entrance. Which MotMots can ride on the roller coaster? Say their names aloud.

You must be **THIS TALL** to ride

Brian
Dimitri

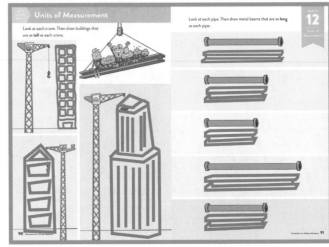

Units of Measurement

Look at each crane. Then draw buildings that are as **tall** as each crane.

Look at each pipe. Then draw metal beams that are as **long** as each pipe.

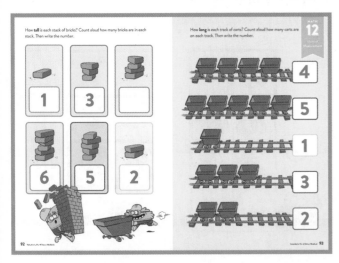

How **tall** is each stack of bricks? Count aloud how many bricks are in each stack. Then write the number.

| 1 | 3 | |
| 6 | 5 | 2 |

How **long** is each track of carts? Count aloud how many carts are on each track. Then write the number.

4
5
1
3
2

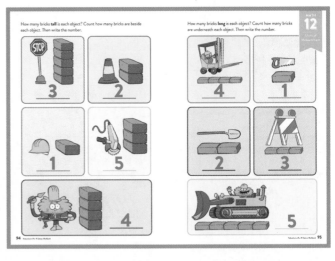

How many bricks **tall** is each object? Count how many bricks are beside each object. Then write the number.

3   2
1   5
4

How many bricks **long** is each object? Count how many bricks are underneath each object. Then write the number.

4   1
2   3
5

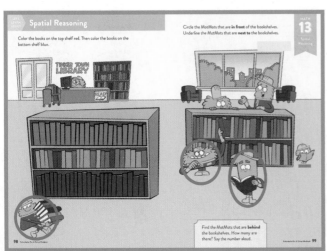

Spatial Reasoning

Color the books on the top shelf red. Then color the books on the bottom shelf blue.

Circle the MotMots that are **in front** of the bookshelves. Underline the MotMots that are **next to** the bookshelves.

Find the MotMots that are **behind** the bookshelves. How many are there? Say the number aloud.

Circle the MotMots that are walking **up** the stairs. Underline the MotMots that are walking **down** the stairs.

Get the MotMot stickers from page 385. Place the MotMots **on** the carpet for story time!

Find the MotMots **in** the reading nooks. How many are there? Say the number aloud.

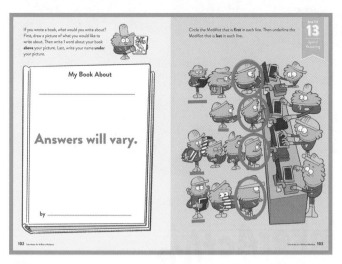

If you wrote a book, what would you write about? First, draw a picture of what you would like to write about. Then write 1 word about your book **above** your picture. Last, write your name **under** your picture.

My Book About

_____

Answers will vary.

by _____

Circle the MotMot that is **first** in each line. Then underline the MotMot that is **last** in each line.

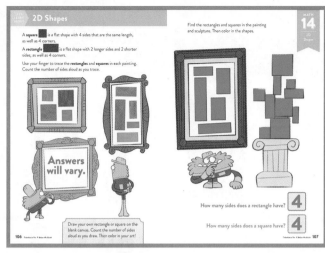

2D Shapes

MATH 14

A **square** is a flat shape with 4 sides that are the same length, as well as 4 corners.

A **rectangle** is a flat shape with 2 longer sides and 2 shorter sides, as well as 4 corners.

Use your finger to trace the **rectangles** and **squares** in each painting. Count the number of sides aloud as you trace.

Answers will vary.

Find the rectangles and squares in the painting and sculpture. Then color in the shapes.

Draw your own rectangle or square on the blank canvas. Count the number of sides aloud as you draw. Then color in your art!

How many sides does a rectangle have? **4**

How many sides does a square have? **4**

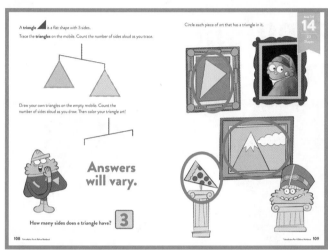

A **triangle** is a flat shape with 3 sides. Trace the **triangles** on the mobile. Count the number of sides aloud as you trace.

Draw your own triangles on the empty mobile. Count the number of sides aloud as you draw. Then color your triangle art!

Answers will vary.

How many sides does a triangle have? **3**

Circle each piece of art that has a triangle in it.

MATH 14

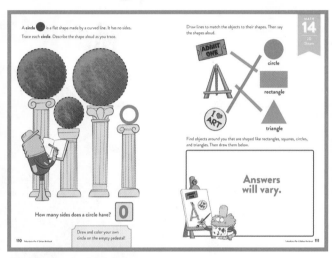

A **circle** is a flat shape made by a curved line. It has no sides. Trace each **circle**. Describe the shape aloud as you trace.

How many sides does a circle have? **0**

Draw and color your own circle on the empty pedestal!

Draw lines to match the objects to their shapes. Then say the shapes aloud.

circle

rectangle

triangle

Find objects around you that are shaped like rectangles, squares, circles, and triangles. Then draw them below.

Answers will vary.

MATH 14

Combining 2D Shapes

MATH 15

Draw a line to complete each shape. Then name each shape aloud.

TINKER TOWN NATURE PATH

Look at the key, and finish the picture by filling in each shape with the correct color.

COLOR KEY

Square:

Triangle:

Circle:

Rectangle:

Look at the key. Finish the picture by filling in each shape with the color that matches its features.

COLOR KEY

A shape that has 3 sides: green

A shape that has no straight sides: yellow

A shape that has 4 sides that are all the same length: brown

MATH 15

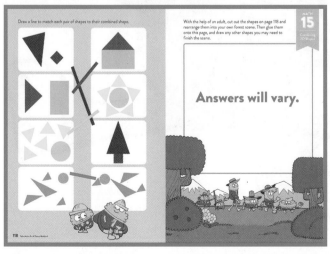

Draw a line to match each pair of shapes to their combined shape.

With the help of an adult, cut out the shapes on page 118 and rearrange them into your own forest scene. Then glue them onto this page, and draw any other shapes you may need to finish the scene.

Answers will vary.

MATH 15

CONGRATS!

You're a TinkerActive Math Champion!

TinkerActive

WORKBOOKS

Pre-K · SCIENCE · AGES 4–5

by Megan Hewes Butler

illustrated by Chad Thomas

educational consulting by Randi House

Odd Dot · New York

Living Things

People are **alive**. They need air to breathe and food and water to grow.

Circle the people at the park.

WELCOME TO TINKERTOWN PARK

You're alive, too! Draw a picture of yourself.

Plants and animals are alive, too. They also need air to breathe and food and water to grow.

Color the plants and animals.

Draw a line to lead the guinea pig to its food and water.

Why does this guinea pig need food and water?
Tell a friend or family member!

Not all things are living. A rock is not alive. It does not need air to breathe, or food and water to grow.

Cross out things that are not alive.

Color the things that are alive.

Can you find any of these things when you look out your window? What else do you see outside that's alive?

Look around your home. Draw two things you see that are alive.

LET'S START! GATHER THESE TOOLS AND MATERIALS.

Glass jar with a wide mouth and a screw-on lid

Nail
(with an adult's help)

Hammer
(with an adult's help)

Small rocks

Dirt

Small plant

Small cup of water

Small piece of
fruit or vegetable

Paper bowls or cups

Small cardboard boxes or shoeboxes

Modeling clay
(optional)

LET'S TINKER!

Most living things can move on their own. Can any of
your materials move on their own, without anything
touching them?

Move your body. Can you use your body to make your
materials move? Are any of your materials living things?

LET'S MAKE: BUG HABITAT!

1. With the help of an adult,
add air to your habitat:
Poke six or more small
holes in the lid of the
glass jar with a hammer
and nail.

2. **Fill** the bottom of
the jar with a layer of
small rocks. Then **add**
a layer of dirt. Then
add a small plant in
the dirt.

3. Add water to your habitat: **Sprinkle** water on the dirt until it is damp. If the dirt dries out a few days later, **do** this again.

4. Add food to your habitat. **Add** a small piece of a fruit or vegetable, like a piece of an apple or a tiny bit of carrot.

5. Hunt for a mealworm, cricket, beetle, or other bug. **Place** it in your jar and screw the lid on tight.

6. Check the dirt and food a few days later, and if the dirt is dry, add a little more water. Pull out any food that's left and replace it with something fresh. **Watch** your bug move and grow!

LET'S ENGINEER!

Brian loves collecting objects while he hikes. This time, he found rocks, a few twigs, a flower, and a button! He wants to organize his objects into living and nonliving things.

How can Brian sort his objects?

Go on a walk and **collect** some living and nonliving things. Then build something to sort them. **Think** about how you sort other small items—what materials would make a good bin for them? How will someone know where to put a living or nonliving thing? Then **sort** your materials! Do you have any living things? If not, **model** one out of clay.

PROJECT 1: DONE!
Get your sticker!

My Body

You are alive. Your body grows and changes.

Start with the baby and trace the line through the life cycle of a person.

baby

child

teen

adult

Circle the things that you can do now that you couldn't do when you were a baby.

Your body parts help you move.

Draw a line to match each action to the body part that moves. Then do the action with your own body!

mouth

hand

eye

hip

foot

Draw your face. Then draw a line to label each part.

(hair) (eye) (nose) (mouth) (ear)

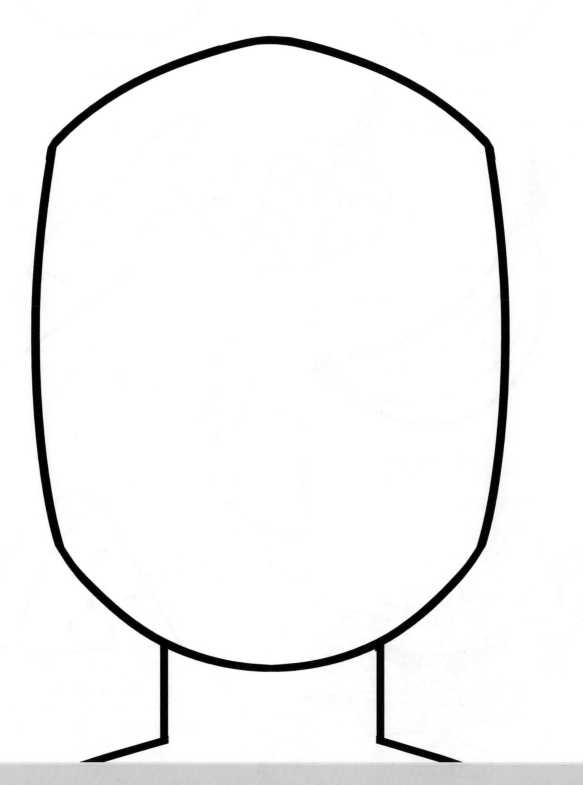

Your body needs food and water to grow. Say the name of each fruit and vegetable aloud. Color the food items you like to eat.

apple

tomato

grapes

carrot

banana

strawberry

watermelon

You eat, sleep, breathe, and move. Animals do, too. Draw a line to match each person and animal doing the same thing.

LET'S START!

Crayons

Paper

6 index cards

Paper bag

Paper plate

 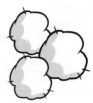

Small items, like:
string, buttons, twist ties, cotton balls, paper clips

LET'S TINKER!

Trace your hand on a piece of paper. Then **trace** a family member's hand. How are they the same or different? Which is bigger? Why?

LET'S MAKE: GO, GO, GO GAME!

1. With the help of an adult, **write** one action word on the front of each index card: hop, skip, crawl, slide, dance, gallop.

2. Draw one place in your home on the back of each card, like a chair, table, or door.

3. Place the cards in the paper bag.

4. Take turns with a friend or family member to play. To start, **pick** two cards. The first tells you what PLACE to go. The second tells you the ACTION to do! (You may hop to a chair, or dance to a table, etc.)

LET'S ENGINEER!

The MotMots made some new friends at school. Dimitri wants to take a picture, but his camera is broken.

How can the MotMots make a picture of their friends instead?

Use your materials to make a picture of your face! **Start** with a paper plate for your head. What can you use to show other body parts, like your eyes, ears, nose, and mouth? What about hair? What other body parts can you show?

PROJECT 2: DONE!
Get your sticker!

Animals

Animals are alive. They grow and change. Baby animals grow up and often look similar to their parents.

Draw a line to match each baby animal to what it will look like when it is fully grown.

Look closely at this baby rattlesnake and baby clown fish.
Then draw what you think their parents might look like.

Animals have body parts to help them move, eat, protect themselves, and communicate.

Look at the body parts of an elephant. Point at the parts that you have, and say the names aloud. Then color the parts that you don't have.

ear

eye

trunk

foot

Circle the mouth on each animal. Then make the sound that each animal makes.

Animals live in **habitats** where they can get the food, water, and shelter that they need.

Draw a line to lead each animal to its home in the forest habitat.

There are many different habitats on the Earth for animals to live in. Draw a line to match each animal to its habitat.

whale

rain forest

polar bear

arctic

toucan

grassland

zebra

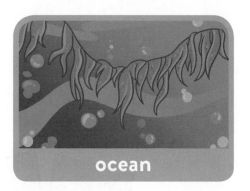

ocean

Take a walk around your habitat at home. Show a friend or family member where you get the food and water that you need!

LET'S START!

Natural materials, like:
leaves, pine needles, sticks, seeds, flowers, bark, grass, rocks

Construction paper

Scissors
(with an adult's help)

Glue stick

Markers

LET'S TINKER!

Look at your materials—which could be found in an animal's habitat? Which would not be? Why? **Sort** the items that could be found in an animal's habitat into a pile. Which kinds of animals might live around materials like these?

LET'S MAKE: SNAKE FAMILY!

1. With the help of an adult, **cut** a sheet of paper into five strips.

2. Bend one strip into a ring and seal it with a glue stick.

3. Bend another strip into a ring that loops through the first ring, and seal it with a glue stick.

4. Continue until all the strips have been used.

5. Use scraps of paper and a marker to add snake eyes and a tongue to your baby snake.

6. Next, **make** a parent snake to go with the baby! How will it be similar or different? How many rings will it use—will it be longer or shorter?

LET'S ENGINEER!

Amelia and Brian found a small round rock that looks like an egg. They are pretending that it might hatch! What pretend animal could be inside?

How can the MotMots make a home for the egg?

Use your natural materials to build a small nest. Which materials could make a soft place for an egg? Which materials could help to hold the nest together?

What would your pretend animal need once it has hatched?

PROJECT 3: DONE!
Get your sticker!

Plants

Plants are alive. They grow and change. Trace the numbers 1, 2, 3, and 4 to put the illustrations in order from first to last.

Plants have many parts to help them live and grow. Say the name of each plant part aloud. Then color the plant.

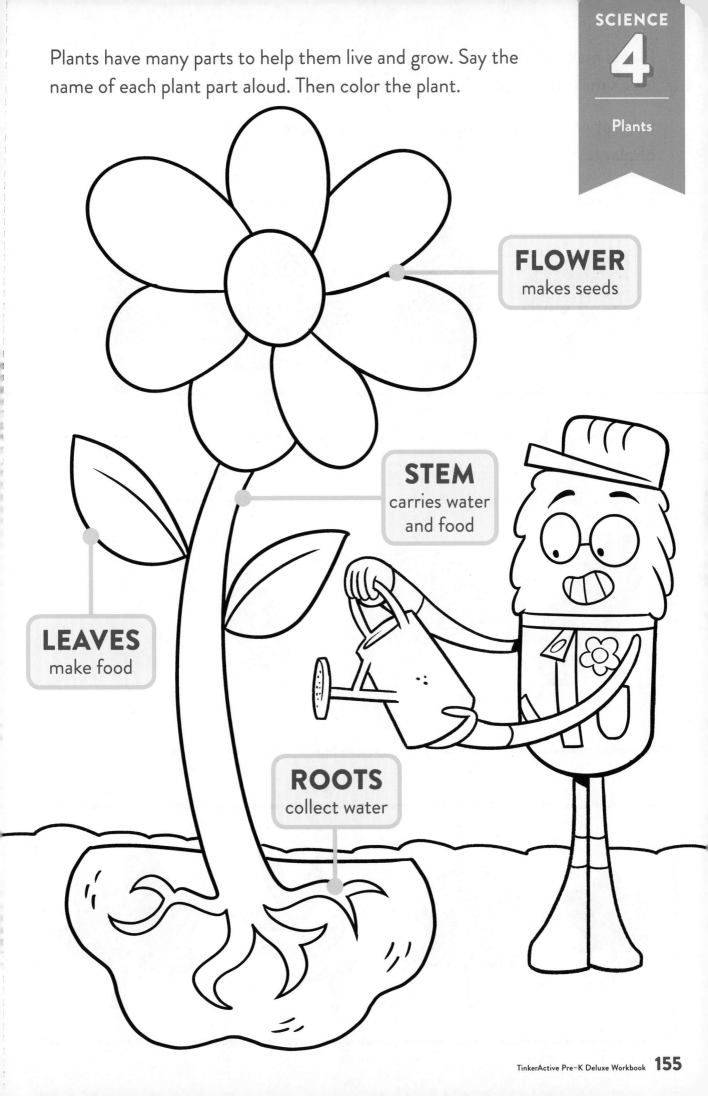

FLOWER
makes seeds

STEM
carries water
and food

LEAVES
make food

ROOTS
collect water

Plants make seeds. Then new plants grow from those seeds. A new plant will look similar to the plant that the seed came from.

Look at each set of leaves. Circle the two that are from the same type of plant.

The MotMots have planted a mystery seed.

Draw the plant you think might grow from it!

Does your plant have flowers? What color are the leaves?

Different types of plants grow in different habitats. With the help of an adult, go on a plant hunt outside. Circle each type of plant you see growing in your habitat.

bush

cactus

moss

grass

fern

tree

flower

vine

Find a leaf. Hold it down with one hand, and trace it with the other. Color in your tracing to match the leaf.

Hunt for another leaf from a different type of plant! What makes the leaves different?

LET'S START!

GATHER THESE TOOLS AND MATERIALS.

Natural materials, like:
leaves, pine needles, sticks, seeds, flowers, bark, grass, rocks

White paper

Crayons

Paint

Rubber bands or tape

LET'S TINKER!

Use the natural materials from outside to make a model of a plant. **Show** roots to collect water. **Show** a stem to carry water and food. **Show** leaves to make food. **Show** a flower to make seeds.

LET'S MAKE: LEAF RUBBINGS!

1. **Find** a few leaves of different shapes and sizes.

2. **Lay** a leaf flat on a table. **Make** sure that the smooth top side is facing down, so that the bumpy veins on the back side are facing up.

3. Lay a sheet of paper on top.

4. Slowly **rub** over the leaf with the side of a crayon. **Watch** the leaf appear!

LET'S ENGINEER!

The MotMots want to paint some pictures. They have paint and paper, but they don't have any paintbrushes!

How can they use the things around them from nature to paint?

Put a stick, leaf, or piece of grass in the paint and try to paint on a piece of paper. What happens? What other materials could work? How can you combine materials to make a paintbrush? What happens when you try to use a pine needle or a rock? Or a flower? Which materials work best?

PROJECT 4: DONE!
Get your sticker!

The Earth

We live on planet Earth. It is made of many types of rock.

Draw a line to match the rocks that are the same type.
Then describe their color and texture aloud.

The Earth is covered in land and water. The animals and plants that live on land need air, dirt, and access to water.

Circle the living things that live on land.

Circle the living things that live in the water.

The food, water, and shelter that living things need can be found on Earth. Color the squirrel's food, water, and shelter.

With the help of an adult, read the poem aloud.

The Earth Gives Us What We Need

I live on planet Earth—

it's my favorite place to live!

Here there's water, food, and shelter.

The Earth has much to give.

The oceans give us water,

and rain falls from the sky.

We can grow crops in the fields

and eat from plants nearby!

We cut trees to make wood boards,

and build homes from what's around.

Animals can find shelter, too,

up high or underground.

The Earth gives us what we need—

I can see it's true!

There's water, food, and shelter

here for me and you.

Draw a line to match each item to the place that it comes from.

food

water

shelter

LET'S START!

GATHER THESE TOOLS AND MATERIALS.

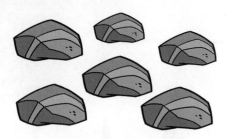
6 or more rocks

Construction paper

Scissors
(with an adult's help)

Pan or large bowl

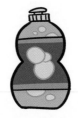
Liquid soap

Modeling clay

LET'S TINKER!

Look closely at your rocks. Can you find some that are a similar shape? What about a similar color? Or size? How many different kinds of rocks did you find?

Put them in a row from smallest to largest.

LET'S MAKE: SWIMMING FISH!

1. With the help of an adult, **cut** a small fish shape out of a piece of construction paper. It should be about as long as your finger.

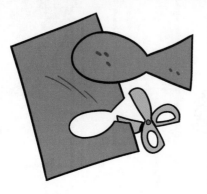

2. Cut a V-shaped slot in the fish's tail.

3. Fill a pan or bowl with water about as deep as your thumb.

4. Place the fish in the water so that it floats.

5. Squirt one drop of liquid soap into the water right behind the fish, by the slot in its tail.

6. Watch it swim! You can **refill** the container with fresh water and try again.

LET'S ENGINEER!

A squirrel keeps sneaking into Amelia's house. She thinks the squirrel is looking for food, water, or shelter.

How can she show the squirrel where it can get food, water, and shelter outside her house?

Make models of the things a squirrel needs to live. Where will it get food: nuts from a tree or vegetables from someone's garden? Where will it get the water it needs: from a lake or the rain? Where will it get the shelter it needs: a hole in a tree or a burrow underground?

PROJECT 5: DONE!
Get your sticker!

The Sky

The sun, moon, stars, and clouds are in the sky. Touch the picture of each object and describe what it looks like. Then trace each name.

Go outside or look out your window. Draw a picture of what you see in the sky.

What color is the sky?

The sun is a star—a hot ball of burning gas. It rises and sets each day. During the day it gives us light and heat.

Circle the things you do during the day.

The moon can often be seen at night. Without the sun, the sky becomes darker and it is cooler outside.

Circle the things you do during the night.

Groups of stars in a pattern form a **constellation**.

Trace the line to complete the constellation of Leo the Lion.

The sun is the closest star to our planet. But at night, when the sun has set, we can often see other stars.

Start here

Clouds are made up of drops of water and ice so tiny that they float in the air. Clouds are always moving and changing.

What pictures do you see in the clouds? Draw faces to make them into animals.

Look outside. What pictures do you see in the clouds?

LET'S START!

GATHER THESE TOOLS AND MATERIALS.

Paper

Newspaper

Construction paper

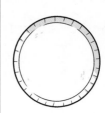
Paper plate

Paint
(red, orange, and yellow)

Plastic wrap

10 or more mini marshmallows

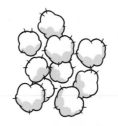
10 or more cotton balls

10 or more pieces of uncooked spaghetti

LET'S TINKER!

Use your materials to make clouds. They are always moving and changing! What shapes can you make? Do they move and change when you blow on them?

LET'S MAKE: BURNING SUN!

1. **Lay** your paper plate on newspaper and pour red, orange, and yellow paint on top.

2. **Lay** a sheet of plastic wrap on top of the plate.

3. Smoosh the paint to mix and move it around.

4. Peel off the plastic wrap and let your sun dry.

LET'S ENGINEER!

The MotMots are stargazing. They are making up their own constellations in the stars. Frank sees an alligator! He points at it to show his friends, but they can't quite tell where he's pointing.

How can Frank share the shape of his constellation with his friends?

Use your marshmallows, spaghetti, and cotton balls to design and make your own constellation to share with your friends and family! What shapes, patterns, and pictures can you make?

PROJECT 6: DONE!
Get your sticker!

The weather describes what the air outside is like. The weather is always changing.

Color the picture of weather that is rainy.

Color the picture of weather that is snowy.

Color the picture of weather that is sunny.

Color the picture of weather that is cloudy.

What do you like to do outside in each type of weather?

Circle the items that each MotMot should wear or use.

RAINY

SUNNY

SNOWY

WINDY

Observe the weather outside your window, and draw a picture of what you see.

What clothes do you need to wear to go outside? Add yourself and your clothes to the drawing.

Listen carefully. Can you hear any sounds from the weather today?

Use the stickers on page 387 to complete the snowman.

Not all places have snow! Have you ever seen snow? What do you like to do in the snow?

LET'S START!

GATHER THESE TOOLS AND MATERIALS.

10 or more cotton swabs

Clear glass vase (or jar or cup)

Shaving cream

3 small bowls

Food coloring

Small eyedropper (or ¼ teaspoon scoop)

1 cotton ball

Piece of foil

3–5 rubber bands

Piece of paper

2 or more napkins

LET'S TINKER!

Design your own snowflake! **Start** by laying out cotton swabs on a flat surface. What patterns can you make? Is your snowflake small or big? What other materials can you use?

LET'S MAKE: COLORFUL CLOUDS!

Make these colorful clouds with the help of an adult.

1. Fill a large clear glass vase halfway with water.

2. Add a few inches of shaving cream to the top.

3. **Fill** three small bowls with about ¼ cup of water each. **Add** five drops of one color of food coloring to each, using a different color for each bowl.

4. **Use** a small eyedropper or ¼ teaspoon scoop to add a few drops of colored water to the top of the cloud.

5. **Add** more drops and colors, and watch what happens when it rains!

LET'S ENGINEER!

Callie was planning to take a walk outside with her dog, Boxer, but it just started raining! Callie has a rain jacket and boots she can wear. But Boxer doesn't have anything to wear to stay dry—and he hates to be wet.

How can Callie keep Boxer dry?

Pretend that your cotton ball is Boxer. **Use** your foil, rubber bands, paper, and napkins to make a covering to keep the cotton ball dry. Which materials would protect the cotton ball in the rain? How can the materials stay on the cotton ball? **Test** your idea by putting the cotton ball with its rain protection under running water in the sink. Did your design work?

PROJECT 7: DONE!
Get your sticker!

Seasons

Read the poem aloud.

Four Seasons

Winter, spring, summer, fall.

Four seasons to count in all.

In the winter, bears hibernate.

But not me—I like to skate.

Spring warms up and flowers grow.

Rain falls a lot. Buds start to show.

Summer brings a break from school.

Flip-flops and shorts keep me cool.

In the fall, the trees go bare.

Get ready for winter—it's in the air!

Trace the name of each season and describe the changes you see. Then circle the season it is now where you live.

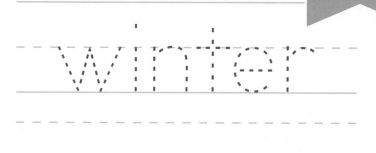
winter

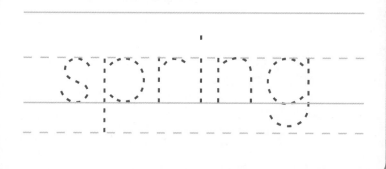
spring

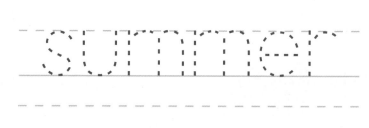
summer

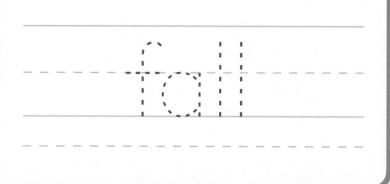
fall

Many animals respond to changes through the seasons. For example, some animals **hibernate** in the winter. This means that when the weather is cold, they go into a deep sleep. In the spring, when the weather is warmer and more food is available, they wake up.

Draw a line to lead the groundhog to its underground burrow so it can hibernate.

Many animals give birth to their babies in the spring. The weather is warm and there is more food for the mothers and babies to eat.

Draw a line to lead the skunk back to her litter of babies.

Plants respond to changes through the seasons. Point to the picture of a tree in the spring and describe what you see. Then draw a picture of what you think it will look like in the summer.

SPRING

SUMMER

People respond to changes through the seasons. Draw a line from each activity to the matching season.

spring

summer

fall

winter

LET'S START!

GATHER THESE TOOLS AND MATERIALS.

Natural materials, like:
leaves, pine needles, seeds, flowers, bark, grass

Duct tape

Paper

Glue

Cotton balls

Crayons

Construction paper

LET'S TINKER!

Make a picture of a tree with your materials. Does your tree change with the seasons? If so, what would it look like in the summer?

How would it look different in the winter? What about spring and fall?

LET'S MAKE: NATURE BRACELET!

1. Ask an adult to help you secure a piece of duct tape inside out around your wrist. (The sticky side should be facing out—not touching your skin.)

2. Take a walk outside and watch what sticks to your bracelet!

3. Find pieces of nature that show the season and stick them on, too.

LET'S ENGINEER!

Every winter, the sheep at Tinker Town's zoo grow thicker wool to keep themselves warm. Callie also needs to dress warmly when it gets cold.

How can she keep warm in the winter?

Draw a picture of Callie on a piece of paper. Then **use** your materials to design things Callie can wear to keep warm when it is cold. What could cover her feet? Her head? Which materials would keep her warmest?

PROJECT 8: DONE!
Get your sticker!

Water & Ice

Water can be found in nature. Point to each place water is found and say the name aloud. Then trace each name.

ocean

rain

lake

river

There is also water in your home. You can use it for drinking, cooking, cleaning, and taking care of plants and animals.

Circle the places where you see water.

Hunt around your home and find three places with water.

Water is a **liquid**. Liquids have no shape—they become the shape of whatever they are in. Use a blue crayon to color each container so it looks full of water.

Juice and milk are also liquids.

Draw what you like to drink in each MotMot's glass.

When water gets very cold, it freezes and becomes ice. Ice is a **solid**. Solids are hard and have a shape.

Circle each picture that shows ice and say the name aloud.

ice cube

iceberg

rain

waterfall

icicle

When ice gets warmer, it melts and becomes water again. Draw what will happen to the MotMots' ice sculptures on a hot day.

BEFORE

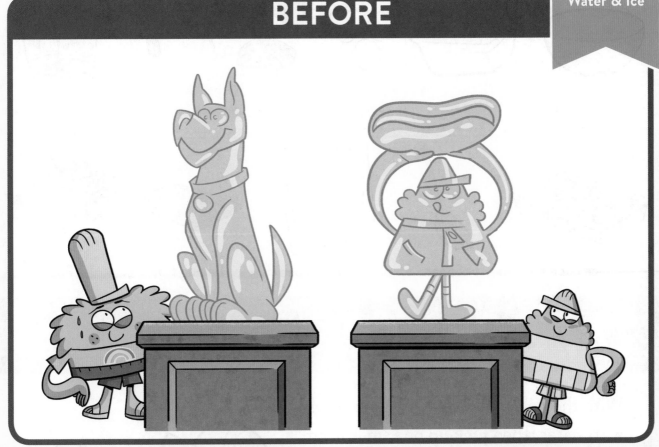

AFTER

LET'S START!

Large bowl

Water

Small water-safe items, like:
a paper clip, cotton ball, pinecone, rock, leaf

Washable paint

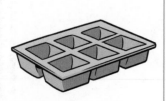
Old ice cube tray

Spoon

Thick paper

Baking tray

Foil

LET'S TINKER!

With the help of an adult, **fill** your bowl halfway with water. Then **pick up** one small item. Do you think it will sink or float? **Make** a prediction and then drop the item into the bowl. Were you correct? **Make** predictions for all your items and then test them out!

LET'S MAKE: FROZEN SOLID PAINT CUBES!

1. With the help of an adult, **squeeze** washable paint into an ice cube tray so each cube is about half full.

2. Add water to each cube and stir with a spoon.

3. Put the tray in the freezer.

4. Place a piece of thick paper onto a baking tray.

5. When the cubes are fully frozen, **pop** them out on the paper and move them around on the paper to make a picture!

LET'S ENGINEER!

Frank and Dimitri entered Tinker Town's winter ice sculpture competition. This year's challenge is to break the mold and make interesting shapes out of ice!

How can they make ice into new shapes?

Make your own ice mold out of a piece of foil. **Try** wrapping the foil around a small toy or around your hand. What new shape can you make? Then, with the help of an adult, **fill** it with water and put it in the freezer. The next day, **take out** your ice sculpture!

PROJECT 9: DONE!
Get your sticker!

Taking Care of the Earth

People, animals, and plants live on the Earth. It's our job to take care of it! One way to keep the Earth clean is to put garbage in trash bins.

Draw a line from each piece of garbage to the trash bin.

When garbage isn't put in trash bins, it can sometimes get into the oceans.

Cross out the things that don't belong in the ocean.

Another way to take care of the Earth is to recycle. Recycling happens when something that has been used is changed into something that can be used again.

Draw a line from each piece of glass to the glass recycling bin.

Draw a line from each piece of paper to the paper recycling bin.

With the help of a family member, find some used paper that you can recycle!

Another way to take care of the Earth is to fix things that are broken instead of throwing them away.

Draw a line from each broken object to the object that can fix it.

You can also take care of the Earth by reusing things instead of throwing them away. Draw a line to match each object to a way that it could be used again.

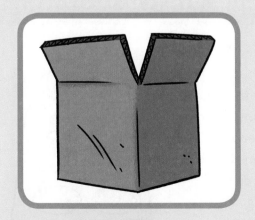

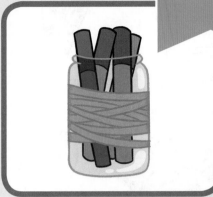

LET'S START!

GATHER THESE TOOLS AND MATERIALS.

Paper

Broken crayons

Assorted items, like:
string, a glass cup, a plastic toy

Muffin tin

Oven mitt

Scissors
(with an adult's help)

Toilet paper tube

Glue

LET'S TINKER!

Look closely at your materials. Are any of them made from recyclable materials? **Draw** four signs: one each for glass, plastic, metal, and paper. Then **sort** your materials into piles based on what they are made of.

LET'S MAKE: RECYCLED CRAYONS!

1. **Peel** the labels off the broken crayons.

2. In a muffin tin, **fill** a cup to the top with broken crayons. (If you have enough crayons to fill more cups, keep going!)

3. With the help of an adult, use an oven mitt to **place** your muffin tin in a 275-degree oven.

4. With the help of an adult and an oven mitt, **take** the muffin tin out of the oven once the crayons are completely melted (about 10 to 15 minutes).

5. Let the crayons cool overnight before using them. (Or cool them for 20 minutes on a cooling rack and then 10 minutes in the fridge.)

LET'S ENGINEER!

Oh no! Callie's toy robot broke. She knows that one way to take care of the Earth is to fix things that are broken instead of throwing them away.

How can she make a new head and arms to fix her robot?

Build your own robot! **Start** with a toilet paper tube. **Use** paper, scissors, glue, and other materials to add a head and arms to your robot. What other parts can you add? Does your robot have buttons, antennae, or wheels?

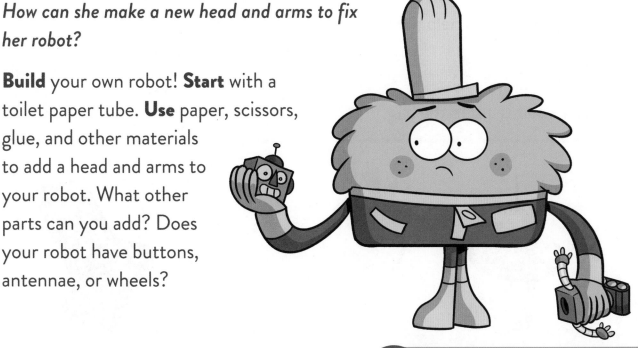

PROJECT 10: DONE!
Get your sticker!

You can use your senses to learn more about the world around you. Read the poem aloud.

WHAT'S INSIDE?

I wonder what's inside this bag.
I know just what to do!
I can touch it, see it, hear it,
and smell and taste it, too.

It feels bumpy in my hand,
and it breaks apart like crumbs.
I see some little white shapes.
And I smell butter—oh YUM!

When I move the bag, I hear it shake.
It goes CRUNCH in my mouth.
It's sweet and salty on my tongue.
My five senses help me out!

Circle what is inside the bag.

You can **see** with your eyes. Eyes come in many different colors.

Look at the eyes of your family or friends. Then color in one eye on the chart for each person. Which eye color did you see the most of?

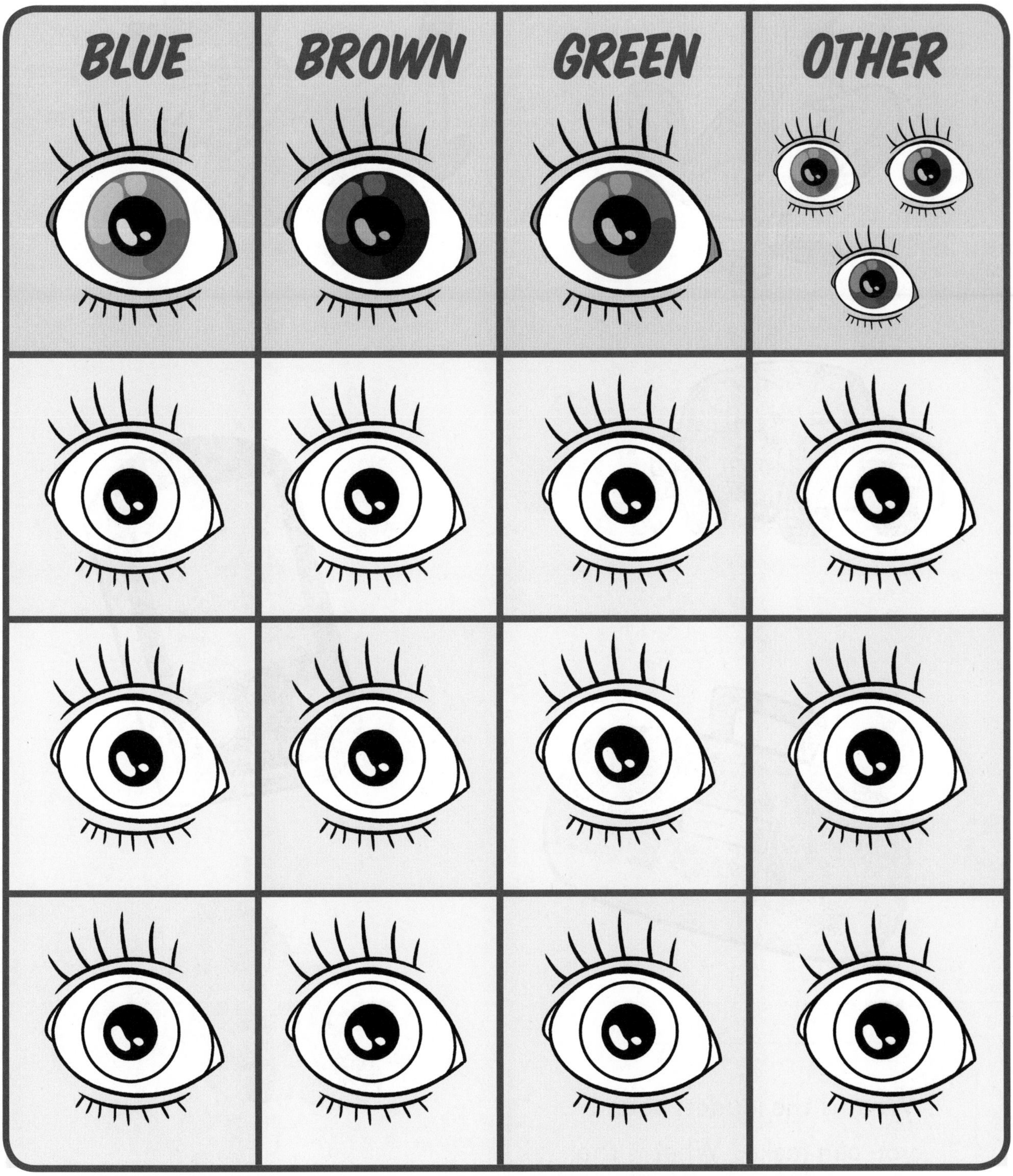

BLUE	BROWN	GREEN	OTHER

Look in the mirror. What color are your eyes?
Color in an eye on the chart for yourself!

You can **hear** with your ears.

Go outside or open a window and listen. Circle the things that you just heard.

What is the loudest sound you can make? What is the softest sound you can make?

You can **touch** with your skin. Hunt for objects that match each description. Then touch and draw them.

cold

smooth

fluffy

sticky

You can **smell** with your nose. Some things smell good and some smell bad.

Circle the things that you like to smell.

You can **taste** with your tongue. When food goes into your mouth, taste buds on your tongue tell you if the food tastes sweet, salty, sour, or bitter.

Draw your favorite foods on the plate. Describe aloud how they taste.

LET'S START!

Small items, like:
rocks, paper clips, cotton balls, uncooked rice

Paper bag

Liquid soap

Cornstarch

Muffin tin
(or ice cube tray)

Liquid food coloring

(Only use liquid food colors. Gel food colors can sometimes stain skin or plastics in the bathtub.)

Jar or plastic bottle with a lid

8 or more coins

LET'S TINKER!

Ask a friend or family member to place one small item into the paper bag. Without looking in, **reach** your hand into the bag. Can you guess what it is just by using your sense of touch? **Take** turns—you can place an item inside for someone else to guess!

LET'S MAKE: BATH-TIME PAINTS!

1. With the help of an adult, **add** 1 tablespoon of liquid soap and 1 teaspoon of cornstarch to each of 4 cups in a muffin tin.

2. With the help of an adult, **add** one drop of a different color of food coloring into each cup and mix the ingredients together.

3. Take the paints into the bathtub! You can **use** a paintbrush or your fingers to start painting. What do the paints look like? How do they feel on your body? Can you smell them?

4. Wash them away!

LET'S ENGINEER!

Dimitri has started a coin collection. He would like to store his coins in a jar, but every time he wants to add a coin, his cat is napping! When he tries to drop a coin into the jar, the loud sound wakes her up.

How can Dimitri place his coins into his jar quietly?

Drop your coins into your jar. What does it sound like? Can you place them in quietly? How can your other materials help? **Try** placing the rocks, uncooked rice, paper clips, or cotton balls in the jar. How do they change the sound of your coins dropping?

PROJECT 11: DONE!
Get your sticker!

Observing & Sorting Objects

There are many ways to describe and sort the objects around you.

Circle the **bigger** object.

Circle the **smaller** object.

Circle the **heavier** object.

Circle the **lighter** object.

Draw lines to match objects that are the **same color**.
Say the name of each color aloud.

Observe the objects around you. Find two objects that you can pick up.
Draw each object below.

Circle the object above that is **bigger**.

Cross out the object above that is **smaller**.

Find two more objects that you can pick up. Draw each object below.

Circle the object above that is **heavier**.

Cross out the object above that is **lighter**.

SCIENCE

12

Observing & Sorting Objects

Find an object that is **soft** and draw it with a pencil.

Find an object that is **hard** and draw it with a pencil.

Find your favorite object and draw it with a pencil. Then circle the words that describe it.

big **small** **heavy** **light** **hard** **soft**

What color is your object? Color your drawings!

LET'S START! GATHER THESE TOOLS AND MATERIALS.

Sheet of sandpaper

Scissors
(with an adult's help)

Colored yarn
or string

Paper plate

Crayons

Glue

Assorted small and colorful items, like:
plastic bottle tops, flowers, leaves

Cotton balls

Markers

LET'S TINKER!

Lay the piece of sandpaper in front of you. With the help of an adult, **cut** pieces of yarn in different lengths. **Lay** the yarn on the sandpaper to make different shapes. Can you make shapes that are big and small? What about round or square?

LET'S MAKE: COLOR COLLAGE!

1. Draw three lines to divide a paper plate into six equal sections.

2. Color each section with crayons: red, orange, yellow, green, blue, and purple.

3. Glue materials with matching colors in each section, such as scraps of paper, yarn, plastic bottle tops, leaves, and more.

4. Look for other items around your home that you could add and glue them on!

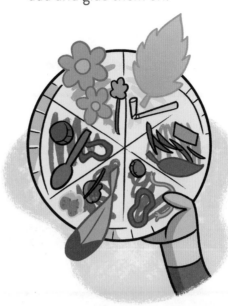

LET'S ENGINEER!

The MotMots made a collection of critters in art class. Amelia made a critter that is big! Brian made a critter that is heavy. They'd like to take them home, but they are TOO big and heavy.

How can they make more critters that are smaller and lighter?

Use your materials, glue, and a marker to make critters that you can carry in your hand. You can also **use** the eyeball stickers on page 387. Which material could make a small critter? Which material could make a light critter? What about soft? How else would you describe them?

PROJECT 12: DONE!
Get your sticker!

Comparing Objects

To **compare**, look at how the objects are the same and how they are different.

Circle the objects that are the **same**.

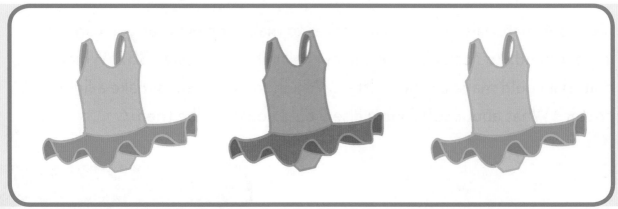

Cross out the object that is **different**.

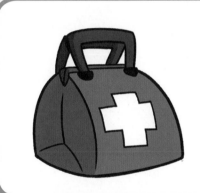  

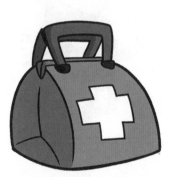

Point to five things in the pictures that are the **same**.

Circle five things in the pictures that are **different**.

Point to five missing pieces in Frank's robot costume. Use the stickers on page 387 to make the pictures the **same**.

Draw a line to match each pair of animals that are the **same type**.

Tell a friend or a family member about your favorite animal. Then ask about their favorite animal. How are they the same or different?

Draw a shape that is the **same**.

Draw a shape that is **different**.

LET'S START!

GATHER THESE TOOLS AND MATERIALS.

10 or more paper cups

Water

Food coloring

Spoon

2 bowls

Milk

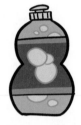
Liquid soap

LET'S TINKER!

Fill two paper cups each halfway with water. Then **use** food coloring to add a few drops of different colors to one cup and stir it with a spoon. What color did you make? **Try** to mix the same color in the second cup! Then, using fresh water, **try** to make it different.

LET'S MAKE: RAINBOW PUDDLES!

1. **Fill** two bowls each with a small amount of milk.

2. Add a few drops of food coloring to the middle of each bowl of milk. **See** if you can make both look the same!

3. Squeeze three drops of liquid soap into the middle of each bowl (on top of the colors) and watch what happens! Do they look different now?

When you are done, pour the soapy milk down the sink drain.

LET'S ENGINEER!

Tinker Town and Bungleburg were racing to see who could build the tallest tower—but both teams were rushing and both towers collapsed! So they decided to work together and build two towers that are exactly the same.

How can the engineers design and build two towers that are exactly the same?

Use your paper cups to build a tower. Then **try** to build another one that is exactly the same. How can you check that it is the same? Does it use the same number of cups? Is it the same height? Did you find any differences?

PROJECT 13: DONE!
Get your sticker!

Making Objects Move

Color the things in the picture that are moving.

Circle the object that is moving **faster** in each picture.

Pushes and pulls can make things move. Pushing moves things away from you.

Circle each MotMot who is **pushing**.

Pulling moves things toward you.

Circle each MotMot who is **pulling**.

Nonliving things can't move on their own, but you can make them move.

Find objects around your home that you can do each action with. Draw the object below that matches each movement.

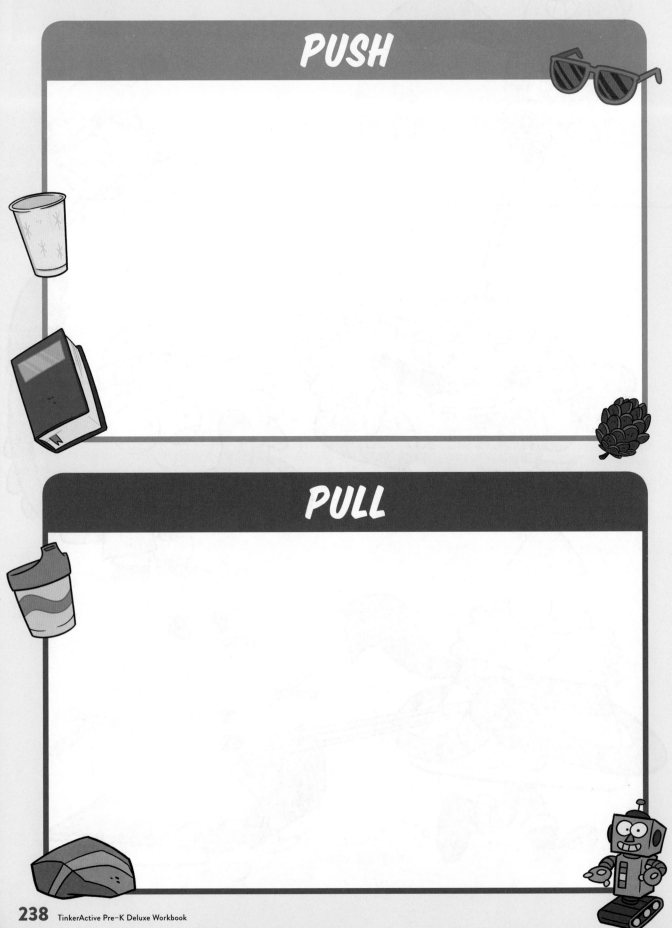

PUSH

PULL

ROLL

DROP

LET'S START!

Baking tray
(or shoebox lid)

Paper

Washable
paint

Small objects, like:
a penny, dried pasta,
a pinecone, a fork

Foil

Cardboard

Rubber bands

Paper clips

LET'S TINKER!

Push and pull to move your materials. Which move in straight lines? Which move in zigzag lines? Which are fast and which are slow? Which can you roll the farthest? **Challenge** a friend or family member to a race!

LET'S MAKE: PUSH-AND-PULL PAINTING!

1. **Lay** a piece of paper inside a tray.

2. **Pour** washable paint into the middle.

3. Take a small object that can get paint on it, like a penny, a piece of dried pasta, a pinecone, or a fork.

4. Push your object through the paint and watch what happens.

5. Then **pull** your object through the paint and watch what happens.

6. Add another color and try again!

LET'S ENGINEER!

Callie and Brian went to play in the snow at Thrill Hill. Callie built the bottom of a snowman at the bottom of the hill. Brian built the top of the snowman at the top of the hill.

How can they move their snowman parts to each other and finish their snowman?

Roll foil into balls to model your snowman parts. Then **use** your materials to build something to move the foil balls. How can you move the snowman parts from one place to another? Can you attach anything to the foil? Can you push or pull it? How else can you move your snowman parts?

PROJECT 14: DONE!
Get your sticker!

Making Objects Change

People can make objects change. Read the poem aloud.
Then color the picture.

I Can Change Things!

I can change things—watch me go!

Pop it. Drop it. Give it a throw.

Mix it, smash it, or shake it now.

Bend or bite it, I'll show you how.

Cut it, shut it, or use some glue.

I can change things, and you can, too!

Animals can make objects change, too.

Draw a line to match each animal to a change it has made.

Heat can make objects change.

Draw a line to match each food to a picture of what happens when it is heated up.

Cold can also make objects change.

Draw a line to match each object to a picture of what happens when it is frozen.

What changes do you feel when you go outside in the cold? Point to different parts of Enid's body and describe what you feel.

Tools can be used to make objects change.

Circle the tool that was used to change each object.

| BEFORE | AFTER | TOOLS |

You can make objects change, too.

Predict what will happen to the objects. Draw your prediction.

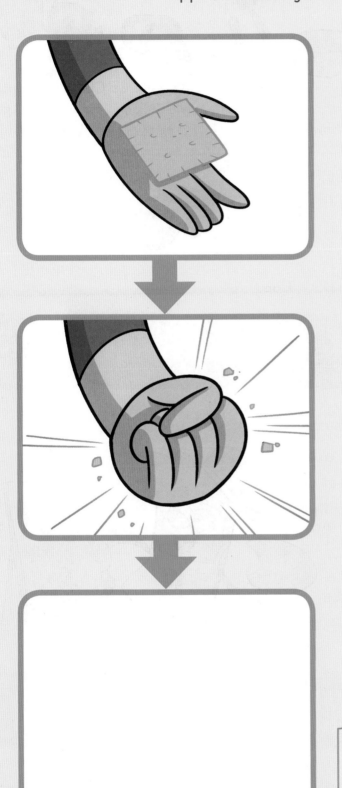

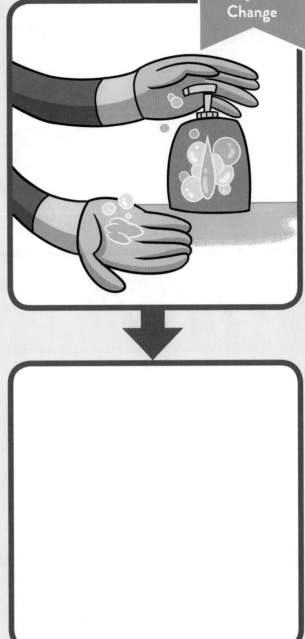

Test your prediction! Go to a
sink and put soap on your hands.
Then rub them together.
What happens? Was it what
you predicted? (Don't forget
to rinse your hands!)

LET'S START!

GATHER THESE TOOLS AND MATERIALS.

 Red, yellow, and blue paint	Paper	2 bananas	 Bowl	Fork and spoon	 1½ cups quick-cooking oats
					Chocolate chips, raisins, or nuts (optional)

 Baking tray	Butter or oil	 Baking soda	Cup	 Foil	 1 cup white vinegar

LET'S TINKER!

Place three small blobs of paint on a piece of paper: red, yellow, and blue. What colors can you make if you mix two of them together with your fingers? What does yellow look like when you mix it with a little bit of red? What about when you mix it with a lot of red? What happens when you mix all the colors together? **Paint** a picture with all your new colors.

LET'S MAKE: BANANA OATMEAL COOKIES!

1. **Peel** two bananas and place them in a bowl. **Mash** them with a fork.

2. **Dump** the oats into the bowl. **Add** a small handful of chocolate chips, raisins, or nuts, if you'd like.

3. Mix all the ingredients together.

4. Grease the baking tray with butter or oil.

5. Place a spoonful of the mixture on the tray and flatten it into a cookie shape. **Do** this again until all the mixture is gone. It will make about twelve cookies.

6. With the help of an adult, **bake** the cookies at 350 degrees for 15 to 17 minutes. Let them cool and then take a bite!

LET'S ENGINEER!

Dimitri loves volcanoes! He loves the hot lava! He loves how the Earth changes! And he wants to see an eruption with his very own eyes.

How can he build his own volcano?

With an adult's help, **scoop** 1 teaspoon of baking soda into a cup. **Place** it on a baking tray. Can you use foil to build the shape of a volcano around the cup?

Pour a bit of vinegar into the baking soda. What do you see? **Try** again by dumping out the cup and then adding more baking soda. What happens when you add a lot of vinegar? How can you make the biggest eruption?

PROJECT 15: DONE!
Get your sticker!

ANSWER KEY

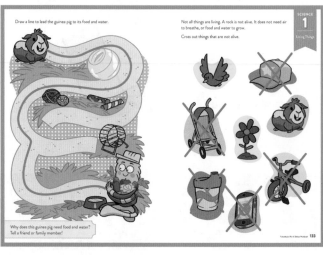

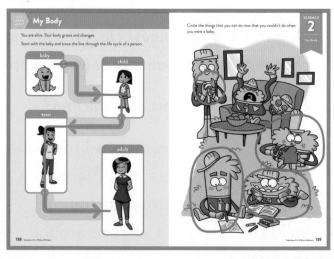

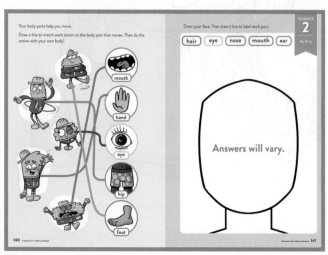

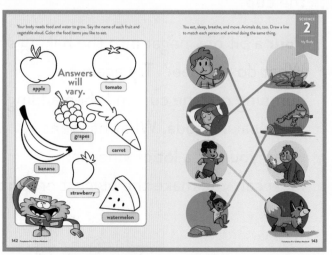

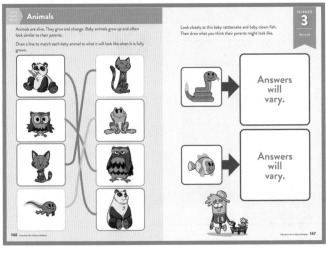

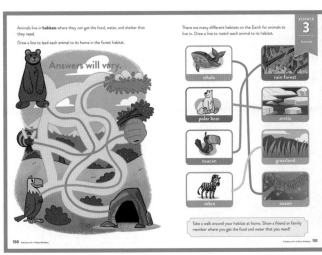
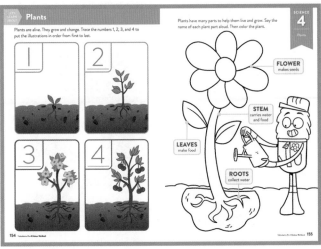

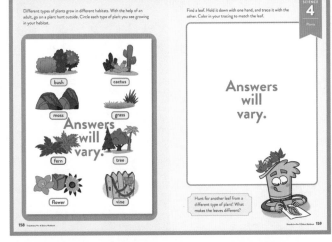

Spread 1 (pages 166-167)

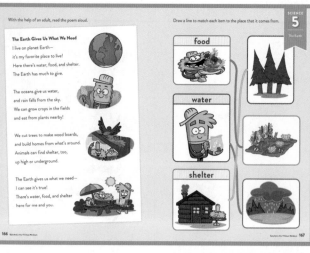

With the help of an adult, read the poem aloud.

The Earth Gives Us What We Need

I live on planet Earth—
it's my favorite place to live!
Here there's water, food, and shelter.
The Earth has much to give.

The oceans give us water,
and rain falls from the sky.
We can grow crops in the fields
and eat from plants nearby!

We cut trees to make wood boards,
and build homes from what's around.
Animals can find shelter, too,
up high or underground.

The Earth gives us what we need—
I can see it's true!
There's water, food, and shelter
here for me and you.

Draw a line to match each item to the place that it comes from.

food

water

shelter

Spread 2 (pages 170-171)

The sun, moon, stars, and clouds are in the sky. Touch the picture of each object and describe what it looks like. Then trace each name.

clouds

sun   moon

stars

Go outside or look out your window. Draw a picture of what you see in the sky.

Answers will vary.

What color is the sky?

Spread 3 (pages 172-173)

The sun is a star—a hot ball of burning gas. It rises and sets each day. During the day it gives us light and heat.

Circle the things you do during the day.

The moon can often be seen at night. Without the sun, the sky becomes darker and it is cooler outside.

Circle the things you do during the night.

Spread 4 (pages 174-175)

Groups of stars in a pattern form a **constellation**.
Trace the line to complete the constellation of Leo the Lion.

The sun is the closest star to our planet. But at night, when the sun has set, we can often see other stars.

Clouds are made up of drops of water and ice so tiny that they float in the air. Clouds are always moving and changing.

What pictures do you see in the clouds? Draw faces to make them into animals.

Answers will vary.

Look outside. What pictures do you see in the clouds?

Spread 5 (pages 178-179)

Weather

The weather describes what the air outside is like. The weather is always changing.

Color the picture of weather that is rainy.

Color the picture of weather that is snowy.

Color the picture of weather that is sunny.

Color the picture of weather that is cloudy.

What do you like to do outside in each type of weather?

Spread 6 (pages 180-181)

Circle the items that each MotMot should wear or use.

RAINY   **SNOWY**

SUNNY   **WINDY**

Spread 7 (pages 182-183)

Observe the weather outside your window, and draw a picture of what you see.
What clothes do you need to wear to go outside? Add yourself and your clothes to the drawing.

Answers will vary.

Listen carefully. Can you hear any sounds from the weather today?

Use the stickers on page 387 to complete the snowman.

Answers will vary.

Not all places have snow! Have you ever seen snow? What do you like to do in the snow?

Spread 8 (pages 186-187)

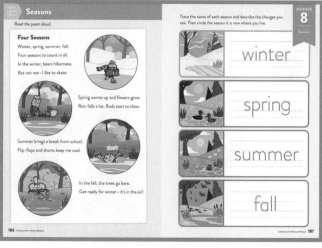

Seasons

Read the poem aloud.

Four Seasons

Winter, spring, summer, fall.
Four seasons to count in all.
In the winter, bears hibernate.
But not me—I like to skate.

Spring warms up and flowers grow.
Rain falls a lot. Buds start to show.

Summer brings a break from school.
Flip-flops and shorts keep me cool.

In the fall, the trees go bare.
Get ready for winter—it's in the air!

Trace the name of each season and describe the changes you see. Then circle the season it is now where you live.

winter

spring

summer

fall

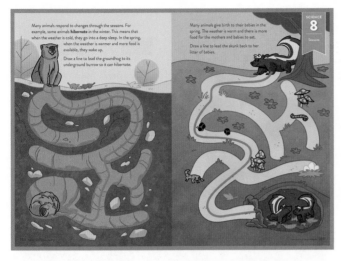

Many animals respond to changes through the seasons. For example, some animals **hibernate** in the winter. This means that when the weather is cold, they go into a deep sleep. In the spring, when the weather is warmer and more food is available, they wake up.

Draw a line to lead the groundhog to its underground burrow so it can hibernate.

Many animals give birth to their babies in the spring. The weather is warm and there is more food for the mothers and babies to eat.

Draw a line to lead the skunk back to her litter of babies.

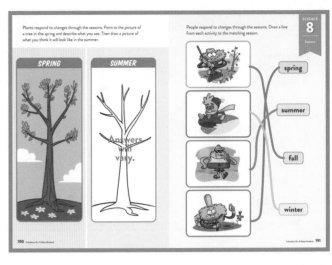

Plants respond to changes through the seasons. Point to the picture of a tree in the spring and describe what you see. Then draw a picture of what you think it will look like in the summer.

SPRING | **SUMMER**

Answers will vary.

People respond to changes through the seasons. Draw a line from each activity to the matching season.

- spring
- summer
- fall
- winter

Water & Ice

Water can be found in nature. Point to each place water is found and say the name aloud. Then trace each name.

ocean | rain

lake | river

There is also water in your home. You can use it for drinking, cooking, cleaning, and taking care of plants and animals.

Circle the places where you see water.

Hunt around your home and find three places with water.

Water is a **liquid**. Liquids have no shape—they become the shape of whatever they are in. Use a blue crayon to color each container so it looks full of water.

Juice and milk are also liquids.

Draw what you like to drink in each MotMot's glass.

Answers will vary.

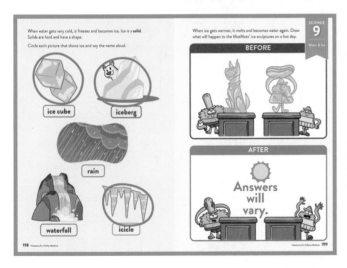

When water gets very cold, it freezes and becomes ice. Ice is a **solid**. Solids are hard and have a shape.

Circle each picture that shows ice and say the name aloud.

ice cube | iceberg

rain

waterfall | icicle

When ice gets warmer, it melts and becomes water again. Draw what will happen to the MotMots' ice sculptures on a hot day.

BEFORE

AFTER

Answers will vary.

Taking Care of the Earth

People, animals, and plants live on the Earth. It's our job to take care of it! One way to keep the Earth clean is to put garbage in trash bins.

Draw a line from each piece of garbage to the trash bin.

When garbage isn't put in trash bins, it can sometimes get into the oceans.

Cross out the things that don't belong in the ocean.

Another way to take care of the Earth is to recycle. Recycling happens when something that has been used is changed into something that can be used again.

Draw a line from each piece of glass to the glass recycling bin.

Draw a line from each piece of paper to the paper recycling bin.

With the help of a family member, find some used paper that you can recycle!

GLASS | PAPER

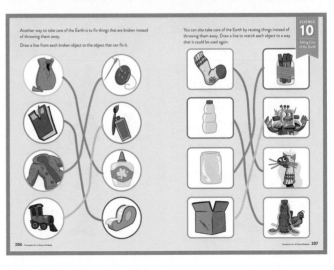

Another way to take care of the Earth is to fix things that are broken instead of throwing them away.

Draw a line from each broken object to the object that can fix it.

You can also take care of the Earth by reusing things instead of throwing them away. Draw a line to match each object to a way that it could be used again.

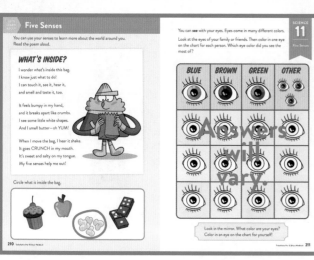

Five Senses

You can use your senses to learn more about the world around you. Read the poem aloud.

WHAT'S INSIDE?

I wonder what's inside this bag.
I know just what to do!
I can touch it, see it, hear it,
and smell and taste it, too.

It feels bumpy in my hand,
and it breaks apart like crumbs.
I see some little white shapes.
And I smell butter—oh YUM!

When I move the bag, I hear it shake.
It goes CRUNCH in my mouth.
It's sweet and salty on my tongue.
My five senses help me out!

Circle what is inside the bag.

You can **see** with your eyes. Eyes come in many different colors. Look at the eyes of your family or friends. Then color in one eye on the chart for each person. Which eye color did you see the most of?

BLUE	BROWN	GREEN	OTHER

Answers will vary.

Look in the mirror. What color are your eyes? Color in an eye on the chart for yourself!

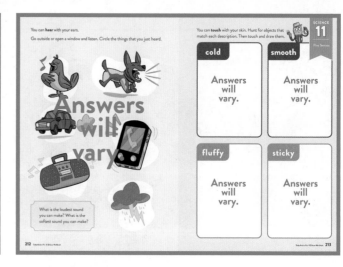

You can **hear** with your ears. Go outside or open a window and listen. Circle the things that you just heard.

Answers will vary.

What is the loudest sound you can make? What is the softest sound you can make?

You can **touch** with your skin. Hunt for objects that match each description. Then touch and draw them.

cold — Answers will vary.
smooth — Answers will vary.
fluffy — Answers will vary.
sticky — Answers will vary.

You can **smell** with your nose. Some things smell good and some smell bad.

Circle the things that you like to smell.

You can **taste** with your tongue. When food goes into your mouth, taste buds on your tongue tell you if the food tastes sweet, salty, sour, or bitter.

Draw your favorite foods on the plate. Describe aloud how they taste.

Answers will vary.

Observing & Sorting Objects

There are many ways to describe and sort the objects around you.
Circle the **bigger** object.

Circle the **smaller** object.

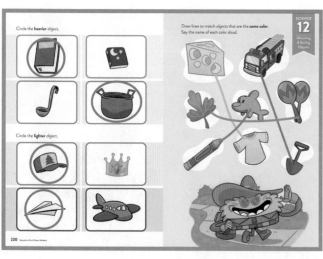

Circle the **heavier** object.

Circle the **lighter** object.

Draw lines to match objects that are the **same color**. Say the name of each color aloud.

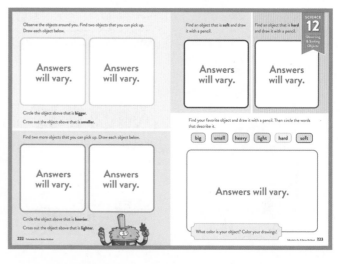

Observe the objects around you. Find two objects that you can pick up. Draw each object below.

Answers will vary. / Answers will vary.

Circle the object above that is **bigger**.
Cross out the object above that is **smaller**.

Find two more objects that you can pick up. Draw each object below.

Answers will vary. / Answers will vary.

Circle the object above that is **heavier**.
Cross out the object above that is **lighter**.

Find an object that is **soft** and draw it with a pencil.
Find an object that is **hard** and draw it with a pencil.

Answers will vary. / Answers will vary.

Find your favorite object and draw it with a pencil. Then circle the words that describe it.

big | small | heavy | light | hard | soft

Answers will vary.

What color is your object? Color your drawings!

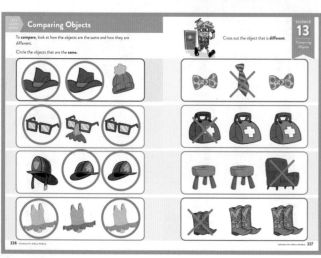

Comparing Objects

To **compare**, look at how the objects are the same and how they are different.

Circle the objects that are the **same**.

Cross out the object that is **different**.

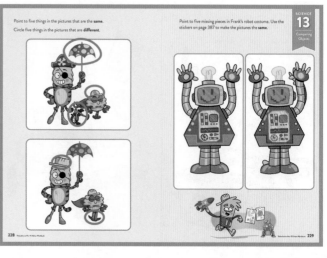

Point to five things in the pictures that are the **same**.
Circle five things in the pictures that are **different**.

Point to five missing pieces in Frank's robot costume. Use the stickers on page 387 to make the pictures the **same**.

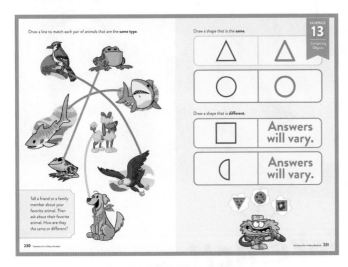

Draw a line to match each pair of animals that are the **same type**.

Draw a shape that is the **same**.

Draw a shape that is **different**.

Answers will vary.

Answers will vary.

Tell a friend or a family member about your favorite animal. Then ask about their favorite animal. How are they the same or different?

Making Objects Move

Color the things in the picture that are moving.

Circle the object that is moving **faster** in each picture.

Pushes and pulls can make things move. Pushing moves things away from you.

Circle each MotMot who is **pushing**.

Pulling moves things toward you. Circle each MotMot who is **pulling**.

Nonliving things can't move on their own, but you can make them move.

Find objects around your home you can do each action with. Draw the object below that matches each movement.

PUSH

Answers will vary.

PULL

Answers will vary.

ROLL

Answers will vary.

DROP

Answers will vary.

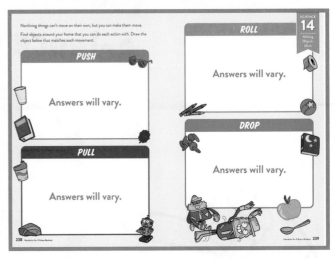

Making Objects Change

People can make objects change. Read the poem aloud. Then color the picture.

I Can Change Things!

I can change things—watch me go!
Pop it. Drop it. Give it a throw.

Mix it, smash it, or shake it now.
Bend or bite it, I'll show you how.

Cut it, shut it, or use some glue.
I can change things, and you can, too!

Animals can make objects change, too.

Draw a line to match each animal to a change it has made.

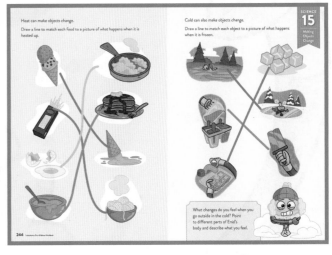

Heat can make objects change.

Draw a line to match each food to a picture of what happens when it is heated up.

Cold can also make objects change.

Draw a line to match each object to a picture of what happens when it is frozen.

What changes do you feel when you go outside in the cold? Point to different parts of Enid's body and describe what you feel.

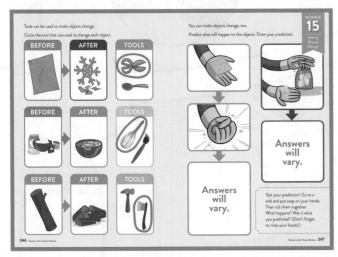

Tools can be used to make objects change. Circle the tool that was used to change each object.

BEFORE	AFTER	TOOLS

You can make objects change, too. Predict what will happen to the objects. Draw your prediction.

Answers will vary.

Answers will vary.

Test your prediction! Go to a sink and put soap on your hands. Then rub them together. What happens? Was it what you predicted? (Don't forget to rinse your hands!)

CONGRATS!

You're a TinkerActive Science Champion!

TinkerActive WORKBOOKS

PRE-K · ENGLISH LANGUAGE ARTS · AGES 4–5

by Megan Hewes Butler

illustrated by Pat Lewis

educational consulting by Randi House

Odd Dot · New York

With the help of an adult, read the poem. Then follow the instructions in the last line of the poem.

Alphabet Game

Letters, letters in a row.
Read them fast, then read them slow.
Point to each letter as you go!

Now use the alphabet, just the same,
To help you play this little game:
Find the letters that spell your name!

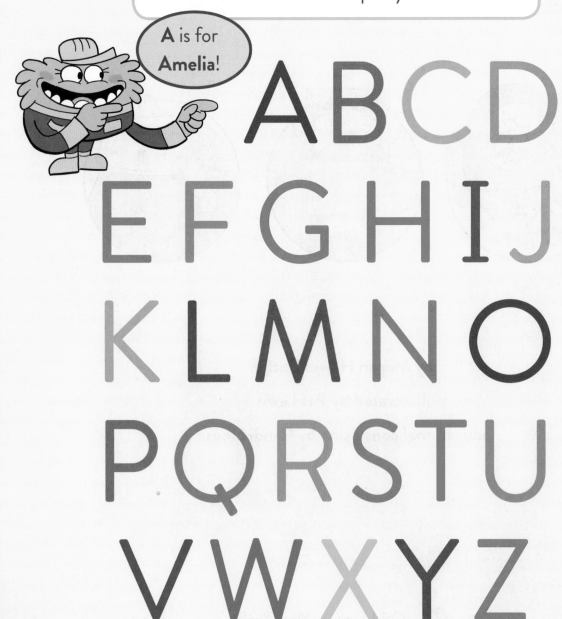

A is for Amelia!

ABCD
EFGHIJ
KLMNO
PQRSTU
VWXYZ

Aa

Trace the uppercase and lowercase letters with your finger. Then trace and write the letters with a pencil. Start a new letter at each dot.

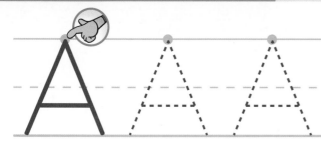

Say it aloud: **Apple** starts with the /a/ sound.
Color all the apples.

Bb

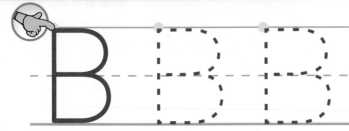

Trace the uppercase and lowercase letters with your finger.

Then trace and write the letters with a pencil. Start a new letter at each dot.

B B B

b b b

Say it aloud: **Ball** starts with the **/b/** sound. Draw a line between the matching letters.

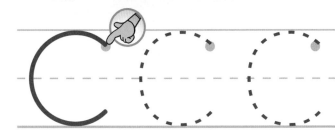

Trace the uppercase and lowercase letters with your finger.

Then trace and write the letters with a pencil. Start a new letter at each dot.

C ⁙ ⁙ C ⁙ C ⁙

c ⁙ c ⁙ c ⁙

Say it aloud: **Car** starts with the /c/ sound.

Circle each car with a **C** or **c**.

Dd

Trace the uppercase and lowercase letters with your finger.

Then trace and write the letters with a pencil. Start a new letter at each dot.

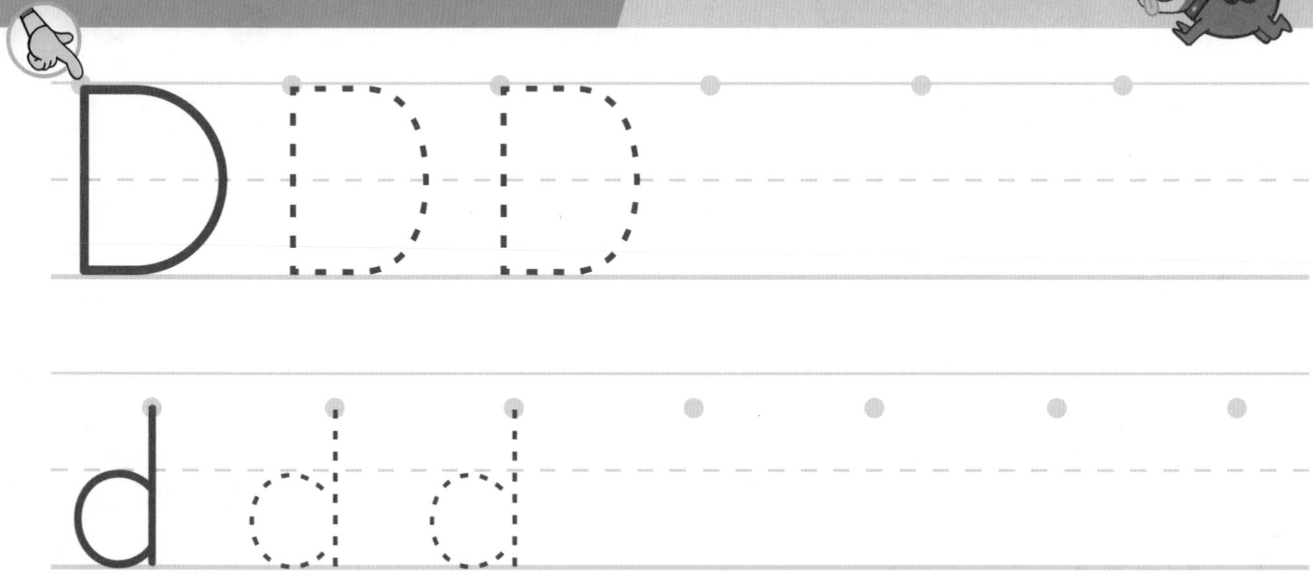

D D D D

d d d

Say it aloud: **Dog** starts with the **/d/** sound.

Draw a line to lead the dog along the path to his doghouse.

Meet the MotMots!

This is Amelia. Her favorite letter is **A**. Circle all the blocks with the letter **A**.

Point to the pictures on the blocks that start with the /a/ sound and say their names aloud.

LET'S START! GATHER THESE TOOLS AND MATERIALS.

 Plastic garbage bag	 Scissors (with an adult's help)	 Shaving cream	 Glue	 3 paper cups
 Food coloring	Spoon	 Plastic freezer bag	 Paper plates	Stapler

LET'S TINKER!

With the help of an adult, **make** a workspace that can get messy by cutting open a garbage bag and laying it flat on a table. **Spray** a pile of shaving cream onto the middle. What does it feel like when you touch it? How does it move when you drag your hands through it? **Rub** it over the garbage bag to make a flat surface and draw in it with your fingers. What letters can you write?

LET'S MAKE: STICKY WINDOW ART!

1. Squeeze glue into 3 paper cups, about as deep as your fingertip in each.

2. Choose 3 colors and add 1–3 drops of food coloring into each cup. **Mix** each with a spoon.

3. Lay a plastic freezer bag on a table and smooth it out so it's flat.

4. **Scoop** some colored glue onto the plastic bag. The spoon can help you move it around to create designs. You can **make** letters, shapes, or other pictures!

5. **Let** your designs dry overnight. Then **peel** them off the plastic and stick them on a window!

LET'S ENGINEER!

The MotMots are having a Letter B Picnic for Brian's birthday! They must each bring foods that start with the letter B. Brian was carrying blackberries, broccoli, bacon, and a bagel, but his plate tore into two pieces!

How can Brian carry his food with a paper plate that is torn in half?

With the help of an adult, **cut** your paper plate in half. Can you use the pieces to carry items? **Try** stacking or bending the pieces. **Try** putting the pieces back together in a new way, like making a basket. **Use** a stapler to hold your design together, and add any necessary materials to make your new object work. Then **find** foods in your own kitchen that start with the letter B and test out your carriers!

PROJECT 1: DONE!
Get your sticker!

Trace the uppercase and lowercase letters with your finger.

Then trace and write the letters with a pencil. Start a new letter at each dot.

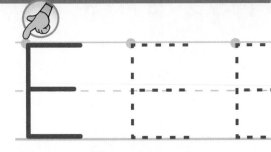

Say it aloud: **Egg** starts with the **/e/** sound.

Draw a design on each egg.

Ff

Trace the uppercase and lowercase letters with your finger.

Then trace and write the letters with a pencil. Start a new letter at each dot.

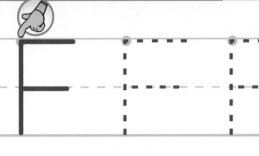

Say it aloud:
Fox starts with the **/f/** sound.

Color all the foxes.

Meet the MotMots!

This is Brian. He loves playing with his pet fish. Start at the dot and trace each line that shows where his pet swam.

Gg

Trace the uppercase and lowercase letters with your finger.

Then trace and write the letters with a pencil. Start a new letter at each dot.

G G G

g g g

Say it aloud: **Goat** starts with the /g/ sound.

Draw a line to lead the goat along the path to the grass.

H h

Trace the uppercase and lowercase letters with your finger.

Then trace and write the letters with a pencil. Start a new letter at each dot.

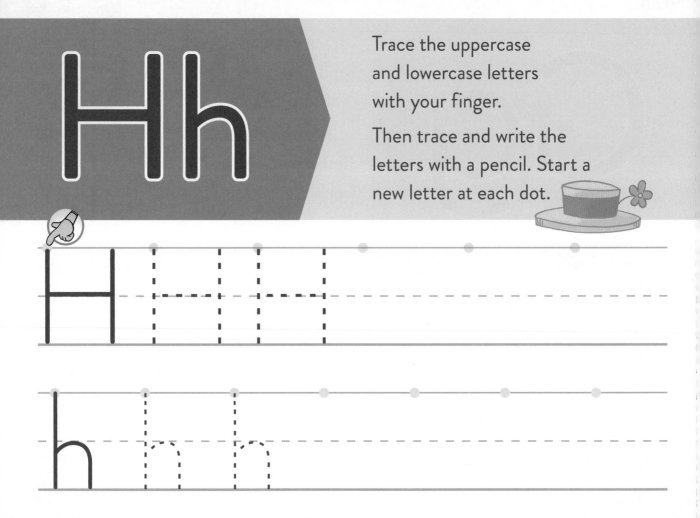

Say it aloud: **Hat** starts with the **/h/** sound.
Color each hat with an **H** or **h**.

Meet the MotMots!

This is Callie. She loves to build paper houses. Start at the dot and trace the path to each house.

LET'S START!

 Plastic garbage bag	 Scissors (with an adult's help)	Salt	Cotton swab	Flour	Water	1 large bowl and 3 small bowls
Food coloring	Spoon	Paper plate	 4 pieces of paper	 Crayons or markers	Tape	

LET'S TINKER!

With the help of an adult, **make** a workspace that can get messy by cutting open a garbage bag and laying it flat on a table. **Pour** about a cup of salt onto your workspace. **Use** your finger to move it around. **Try** pushing, dragging, and twirling your fingers. Also **try** using a cotton swab. How does the salt move and change? What letters, shapes, and pictures can you make?

LET'S MAKE: MICROWAVE PUFF-UP PAINT!

1. **Mix** 1 cup of flour, 1 cup of water, and 1 teaspoon of salt in a large bowl until there are no clumps.

2. **Pour** the mixture into 3 small bowls. **Add** 1–3 drops of food coloring to each.

3. Use a spoon and a cotton swab to paint letters or shapes on the paper plate. **Try** to apply a thick layer of paint—it will puff up more.

4. Microwave your art for 20–50 seconds to watch it dry and puff up! (Thin paint will cook quickly, while thicker paint needs a bit longer.)

LET'S ENGINEER!

Callie is building a model of Tinker Town out of paper. There should be a house for each MotMot who lives on her street: Amelia, Brian, and herself!

How can Callie show which house belongs to each MotMot?

Build your own paper houses! Then **write** the first letter of each MotMot's name on their house: **A**, **B**, and **C**. **Make** one house yours by writing the first letter of your name on it! What other houses or buildings can you make for Callie's model?

PROJECT 2: DONE!
Get your sticker!

The Alphabet: Letters I to M

I i

Trace the uppercase and lowercase letters with your finger.

Then trace and write the letters with a pencil. Start a new letter at each dot.

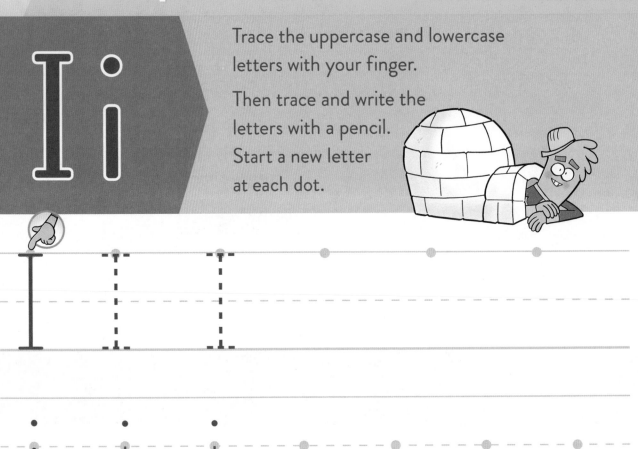

Say it aloud: **Igloo** starts with the **/i/** sound. Color each block with an **I** or **i**.

J j

Trace the uppercase and lowercase letters with your finger.

Then trace and write the letters with a pencil. Start a new letter at each dot.

J   J   J

j   j   j

Say it aloud: **Jelly** starts with the **/j/** sound. Draw a line to connect each pair of matching letters.

K k

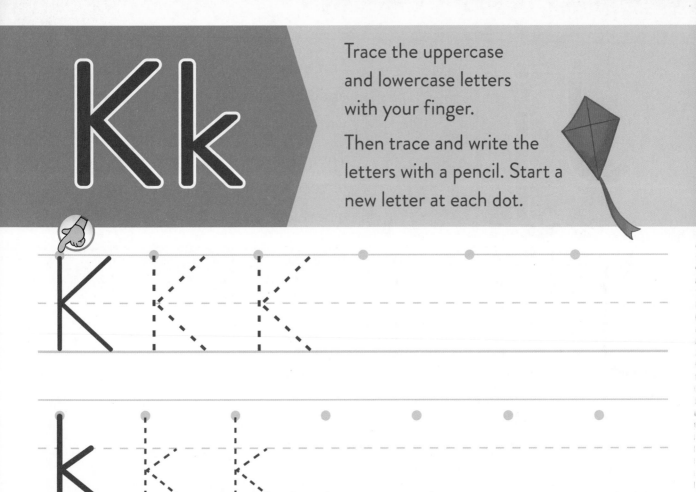

Trace the uppercase and lowercase letters with your finger.

Then trace and write the letters with a pencil. Start a new letter at each dot.

K K K

k k k

Say it aloud: **Kite** starts with the **/k/** sound.
Color all the kites.

Meet the MotMots!

This is Dimitri. He loves drums. Color each drum that has the letter **D**, like his name.

L l

Trace the uppercase and lowercase letters with your finger.

Then trace and write the letters with a pencil. Start a new letter at each dot.

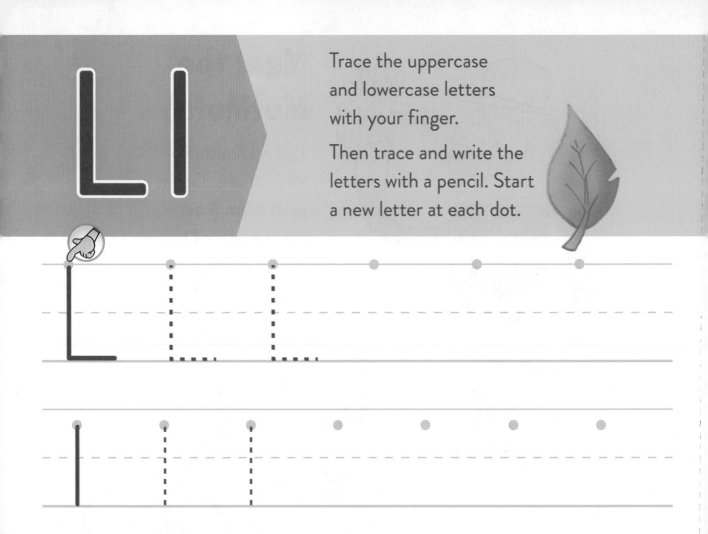

Say it aloud: **Leaf** starts with the **/l/** sound. Say each word aloud. Circle the objects with names that start with the **/l/** sound.

Mm

Trace the uppercase and lowercase letters with your finger.

Then trace and write the letters with a pencil. Start a new letter at each dot.

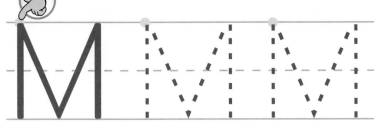

Say it aloud: **Map** starts with the **/m/** sound.

Draw a line along the path to lead Brian to the map.

LET'S START!

About 1 cup of dried beans

Glue

Piece of construction paper

Baking tray

Salt

Watercolor paint and paintbrush

About 30 mini marshmallows

About 30 toothpicks
(with an adult's help)

LET'S TINKER!

Pour your dried beans onto the tray. Can you stack them, roll them, or make them into shapes? **Try** making them into a flat surface and drawing in them. What letters can you draw? **Try** lining them up into rows. What letters can you form?

LET'S MAKE: SPARKLE ART!

1. **Draw** a design on a piece of construction paper with glue. **Add** letters to your design.

2. **Place** your art on a baking tray and sprinkle with salt until the glue is completely covered. **Lift** the paper and shake the excess salt off onto the tray.

3. Let the glue dry overnight.

4. Use a paintbrush and watercolor paint to add color to your sparkly salt designs.

LET'S ENGINEER!

It's snowing in Tinker Town! Dimitri built forts out of snowballs and sticks. Now he wants to build something new.

How can Dimitri use sticks and snowballs to build letters?

Make your own letters with mini marshmallows and toothpicks. **Use** the marshmallows to connect the toothpicks. How can you make straight lines, like the letter **T**? Can you make curved lines, like the letter **O**? Can you make the letters in your name?

PROJECT 3: DONE!
Get your sticker!

Trace the uppercase and lowercase letters with your finger.

Then trace and write the letters with a pencil. Start a new letter at each dot.

N N N N

n n n n

Say it aloud: **Nest** starts with the **/n/** sound. Circle each nest.

Meet the MotMots!

This is Enid. She loves writing her name. Names begin with capital letters. Trace a capital letter **E** on each of her items.

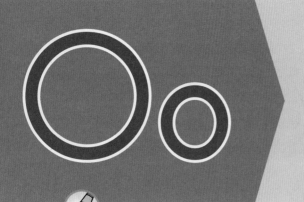

Trace the uppercase and lowercase letters with your finger.

Then trace and write the letters with a pencil. Start a new letter at each dot.

Say it aloud: **Octopus** starts with the *lol* sound.
Color all the octopuses.

Trace the uppercase and lowercase letters with your finger.

Then trace and write the letters with a pencil. Start a new letter at each dot.

Say it aloud: **Pig** starts with the **/p/** sound. Say the name of each object aloud. Circle the objects with names that start with the **/p/** sound.

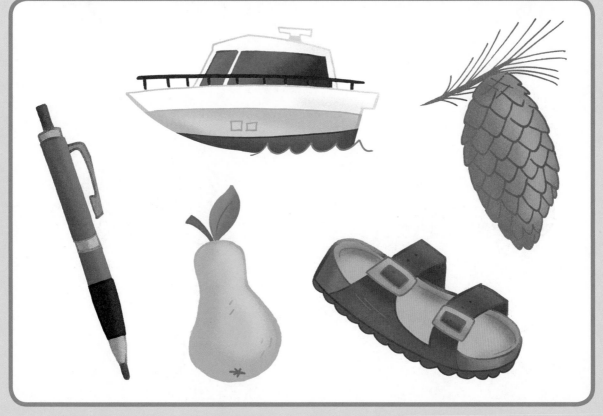

Meet the MotMots!

This is Frank. He loves animals. Trace the missing letters to complete the name of each animal.

dog

pig

cat

fox

Q q

Trace the uppercase
and lowercase letters
with your finger.

Then trace and write the
letters with a pencil. Start
a new letter at each dot.

Say it aloud: **Quilt** starts with the **/qu/** sound.
Draw a line between the matching letters.

LET'S START!

 Paper	Pencil	Washable paint	Small bowls	 Cotton swabs	Cotton ball
 Knife (with an adult's help)	Lemon	 Baking tray	4 or more flat stones	Modeling clay	Permanent marker (with an adult's help)

LET'S TINKER!

Draw lines, shapes, and letters on a piece of paper with a pencil.
Squeeze paint into a small bowl.
Dip a cotton swab into the paint, and make dots on your lines.
Can you make letters with dots?
What happens if you use a cotton ball instead?

LET'S MAKE: SECRET MESSAGES!

1. With the help of an adult, **cut** a lemon in half.

2. Squeeze the juice into a small bowl.

3. Use a cotton swab like a paintbrush to write and draw with the lemon juice on a piece of white paper. You can **write** letters or draw pictures. Your message will be invisible!

4. With the help of an adult, **preheat** an oven and a baking tray to 350 degrees.

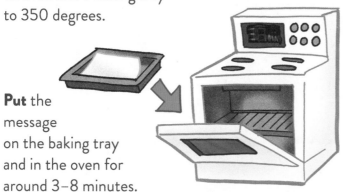

Put the message on the baking tray and in the oven for around 3–8 minutes.

5. Watch carefully and remove the tray when you can see your message. It can change quickly!

LET'S ENGINEER!

Frank wants to teach Callie about the alphabet! But he can't find his alphabet blocks.

How can Frank show the letters and their sounds?

Make your own alphabet blocks! **Look** at your paper, stones, and modeling clay. Could any of these materials be used to show letters? How can you make pictures that start with the sound that each letter makes? Can you make an alphabet toy for each letter of your name? You can **use** the letter and picture stickers on page 389 to help.

PROJECT 4: DONE!
Get your sticker!

Rr

Trace the uppercase and lowercase letters with your finger.

Then trace and write the letters with a pencil. Start a new letter at each dot.

R R R

r r r

Say it aloud: **Rose** starts with the **/r/** sound.
Write the missing **R** and color the roses.

____oses

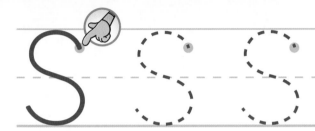

S s

Trace the uppercase and lowercase letters with your finger.

Then trace and write the letters with a pencil. Start a new letter at each dot.

S S S S · · ·

s s s · · · · ·

Say it aloud: **Sock** starts with the **/s/** sound.

Draw a line to match each snake to its sock.

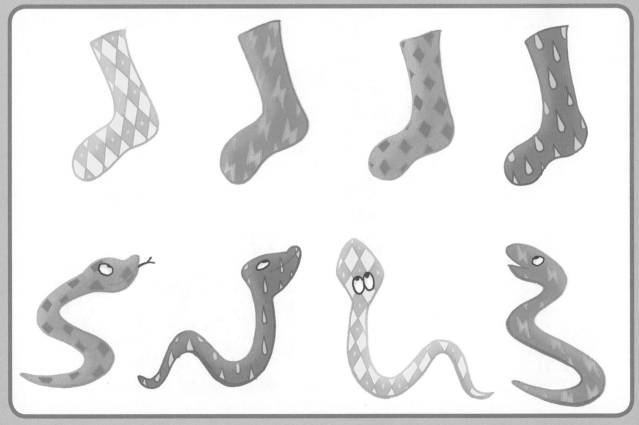

T t

Trace the uppercase and lowercase letters with your finger.
Then trace and write the letters with a pencil. Start a new letter at each dot.

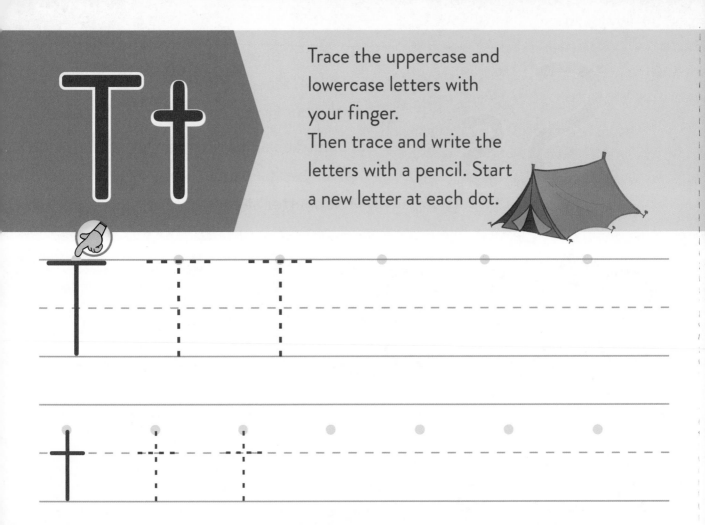

Say it aloud: **Tent** starts with the **/t/** sound. Say the name of each object aloud. Circle the objects with names that start with the **/t/** sound.

U u

Trace the uppercase and lowercase letters with your finger.

Then trace and write the letters with a pencil. Start a new letter at each dot.

U U u u U

u u u u

Say it aloud: **Umbrella** starts with the **/u/** sound.

Draw a line to lead Amelia along the path to the umbrella.

293

The **vowels** in the alphabet are:

A E I O U

Draw a line to match each
uppercase and lowercase vowel.

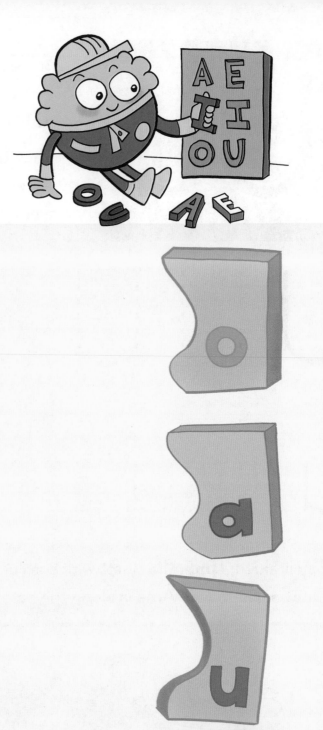

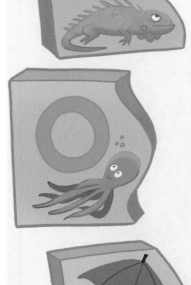

V v

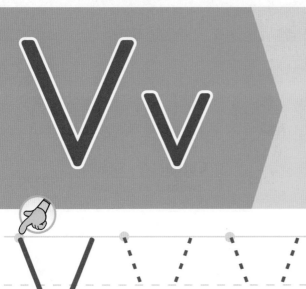

Trace the uppercase and lowercase letters with your finger.

Then trace and write the letters with a pencil. Start a new letter at each dot.

Say it aloud: **Van** starts with the **/v/** sound.
Circle each van with a **V** or **v**.

Flour	Water	Food coloring	Gallon-size resealable storage bag	Tape	Cotton swabs	Small bowl
						Spoon

 10 or more cotton balls	 Baking tray	 5 or more sticks	Scissors (with an adult's help)	Paper	 Crayons

LET'S TINKER!

With the help of an adult, **combine** 1 cup of flour, 6 tablespoons of water, and a few drops of food coloring in the resealable bag.

Seal the top, and then tape the top to ensure that the bag stays closed.

Press and squeeze the plastic bag to move the contents around and mix until there are no lumps.

Lay the bag on a table and use your fingers to draw on top of the mixture.

Try drawing with a cotton swab. Which other materials could you draw with?

LET'S MAKE: COTTON BALL ROCKS!

1. With the help of an adult, **mix** ¼ cup of flour, ¼ cup of water, and 2–3 drops of food coloring in a small bowl with a spoon.

2. Dip a cotton ball into the flour paint until it is fully covered. **Place** it on a lined baking tray. **Cover** as many cotton balls as you can (about 10).

3. With the help of an adult, **bake** at 350 degrees for about 30 minutes, until the cotton ball rocks are hard. **Remove** from the oven and let them cool.

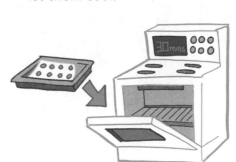

4. Take your cotton ball rocks outside. **Toss** them, smash them, and stack them. You can **make** letters, too! Can you make the first letter of your name?

LET'S ENGINEER!

Enid is getting ready for the Tinker Town Vowel Parade!

How can she make vowel flags that everyone can see?

Gather 5 or more sticks from outside. Then **use** tape, scissors (with the help of an adult), paper, and crayons to make your own flags. How can the paper be attached to the sticks? Do your flags show the vowels uppercase, lowercase, or both? How high can you hold them? **Lead** your own Vowel Parade!

PROJECT 5: DONE!
Get your sticker!

Trace the uppercase and lowercase letters with your finger.

Then trace and write the letters with a pencil. Start a new letter at each dot.

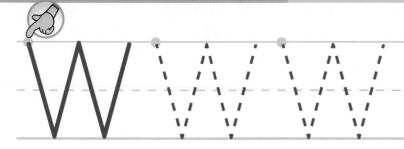

Say it aloud: **Worm** starts with the **/w/** sound.
Trace the lines to lead the worms to the water.

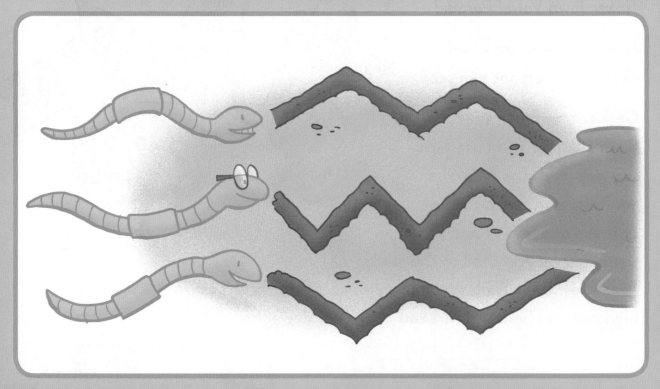

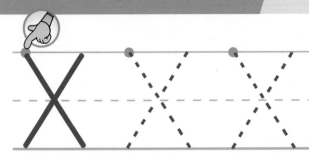

Trace the uppercase
and lowercase letters
with your finger.

Then trace and write the
letters with a pencil. Start
a new letter at each dot.

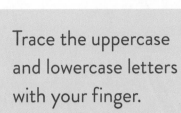

Say it aloud: **Box** ends with the **/x/** sound.

Circle each box with an **X** or **x**.

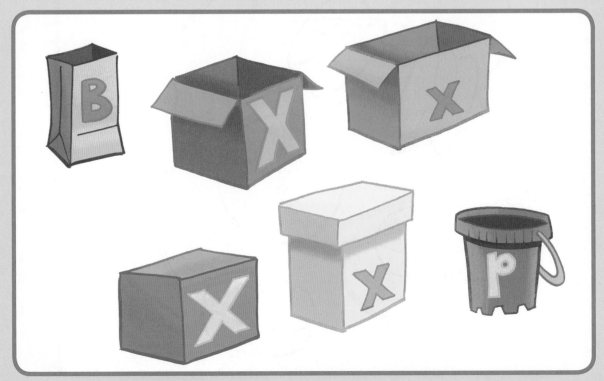

Yy

Trace the uppercase and lowercase letters with your finger.

Then trace and write the letters with a pencil. Start a new letter at each dot.

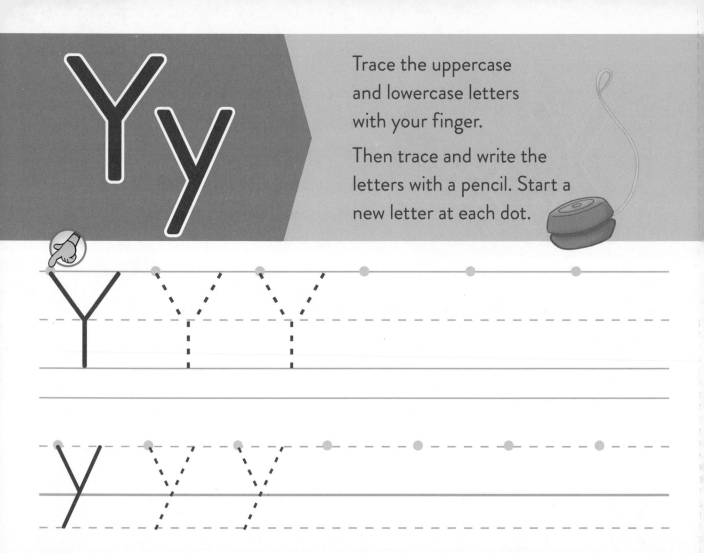

Say it aloud: **Yo-yo** starts with the **/y/** sound.
Color all the yo-yos.

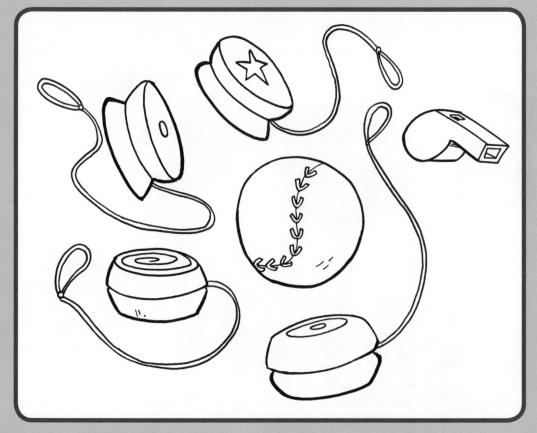

Zz

Trace the uppercase and lowercase letters with your finger.

Then trace and write the letters with a pencil. Start a new letter at each dot.

Z Z Z

z z z

Say it aloud: **Zipper** starts with the **/z/** sound.

Draw a line to move the zipper to the bottom.

Draw a line to lead Enid along the path from the ape to the zebra.
Start at the letter **A**. Say the name of each letter aloud as you go.

Use the letters of the alphabet to spell your name.
Write an uppercase letter for the first letter, like this:

Frank

Write your name
on each item.

LET'S START!

GATHER THESE TOOLS AND MATERIALS.

Dried pasta in various shapes
(wheels, tubes, bow ties, etc.)

Modeling clay

White vinegar

Food coloring

Small plastic container
(about 2 cups size)

Baking tray

Shoebox

Art supplies like:
crayons, markers, glue, scissors (with an adult's help), string, and colored paper

LET'S TINKER!

Make shapes with your modeling clay and dried pasta.
Press the pasta into the clay, roll the clay around the pasta, stand the pasta up in the clay, and make sculptures. Can you make any letter shapes?

LET'S MAKE: PASTA PICTURES!

1. Mix 1 teaspoon of white vinegar and 2–3 drops of food coloring in a small plastic container.

2. Add a large handful of dried pasta to the container. **Use** as many shapes as you have—wheels, tubes, bow ties, or others!

3. Seal the container shut and shake it to mix the color and the pasta.

4. Check inside—if the pasta is covered in color, you are done. If it is not well mixed, **put** the lid back on and shake again. (You can add an extra teaspoon of vinegar to help if needed.)

5. Pour the pasta onto a baking tray and let it dry overnight.

6. Optional: **Repeat** steps 1 through 5 to make more pasta with another color.

7. When the pasta is dry, **use** it to make letters, shapes, and pictures!

LET'S ENGINEER!

Frank is making a Name Collection. He wants to include objects that start with the first letter of his name: F. He already has a fish and a fork.

How can Frank build a container for his Name Collection?

Make your own Name Collection! **Look** at your materials. **Choose** something that could hold many small objects and decorate it. Then **look** around your home to find objects that start with the same letter as your name. **Pick up** an object and say the name aloud. Then **say** your name. Are the beginning sounds the same? If so, **put** it in your container!

PROJECT 6: DONE!
Get your sticker!

Rhyming words have middle and ending sounds that are the same.

Frank's best friend MotBot loves rhyming words—even his name rhymes!
Read each pair of rhyming words and trace the middle and ending sounds.

 pat a cat

 hop on top

 hug a bug

 run for fun

Say the name of each pair of objects aloud, and color the pairs that rhyme.

dog  log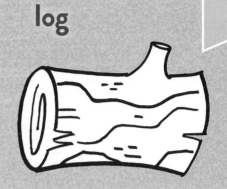

pup  cup

pen  bed

pig  wig

Brian's favorite letter is **B**. He likes balls and boats! Point to each picture below and say the object's name aloud. Circle the objects that start with the **/b/** sound.

Point to something you see near you that starts with the letter **B**.

Trace the first letter of each word with a pencil and read the word aloud. Then draw a line to match each word to its picture.

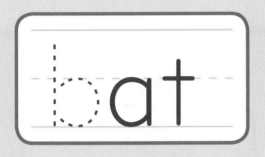
bat

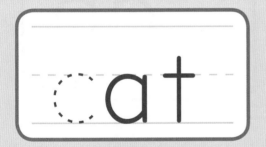
cat

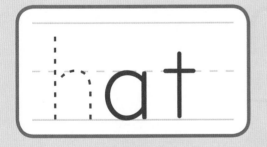
hat

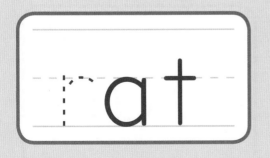
rat

Read the letters below. Then make the sound of each letter aloud.

p f m c

Say the name of each object and listen for the sound of the first letter.
Then write the correct letter to spell each word.

___ an

___ an

___ an

___ an

Read the letters below. Then make the sound of each letter aloud.

d t p h

Say the name of each object and listen for the sound of the first letter.
Then write the correct letter to spell each word.

en

en

en

en

LET'S START! GATHER THESE TOOLS AND MATERIALS.

Small objects like:
a penny, a cotton ball, a piece of dried pasta, a paper clip, or a pinecone

1 large piece of tin foil

10 or more pipe cleaners

3 or more pretzel sticks

4 or more large marshmallows

A handful of cereal in various shapes

Modeling clay

LET'S TINKER!

Arrange your small objects, tin foil, and pipe cleaners to make your own robot! Which materials work best to make a body? Does your robot have arms? Or buttons? What special skills does it have? **Give** your robot a rhyming name!

LET'S MAKE: NEAT ROBOT TREAT!

1. Push a pretzel stick all the way through a marshmallow so that it sticks out of both ends. This is the head and antenna.

2. Add another marshmallow to the bottom of the pretzel. This is the body.

3. Break a pretzel stick in half and use the two pieces to attach 2 more marshmallows as feet.

4. Break another pretzel stick in half and add 2 arms to the body.

5. Push 2 pieces of cereal into the head to make eyes.

6. You can **use** more pretzel sticks and cereal to add more features. Then, **eat** your robot treat!

LET'S ENGINEER!

Frank is building a dome home for his MotBot. A dome has a rounded top, like a ball or a cave. He made a rounded shape with his pipe cleaners, but the dome keeps falling over!

How can he build a dome home for his robot that won't fall down?

Use your pipe cleaners and modeling clay to build your own dome home. How can you make a rounded top? How can the materials be used together to help it stand up? Can you make a robot to fit inside of your dome home?

PROJECT 7: DONE!
Get your sticker!

With the help of an adult, read the nursery rhyme aloud.

Raisin Buns

Three raisin buns in a baker's shop.
Big and round with a cherry on the top,
Along came a girl with a penny one day,
Bought a raisin bun and she took it away.

Two raisin buns in a baker's shop.
Big and round with a cherry on the top,
Along came a boy with a penny one day,
Bought a raisin bun and he took it away.

One raisin bun in a baker's shop.
Big and round with a cherry on the top,
Along came a girl with a penny one day,
Bought the raisin bun and she took it away!

You can make up more nursery rhymes about raisin buns. Start with five raisin buns and count down!

In the nursery rhyme, the words **shop** and **top** rhyme. The words **day** and **away** also rhyme. Say the name of each object aloud. On each shelf, circle the objects with names that ryhme.

Amelia sees a lot of words on her way to the bakery. With the help of an adult, point to each word and read it aloud. Then color the signs.

BUS

WALK

FLOWERS

Draw a line to match each item to the store where Frank can buy it.

Draw a line to match each item to the store where Callie can buy it.

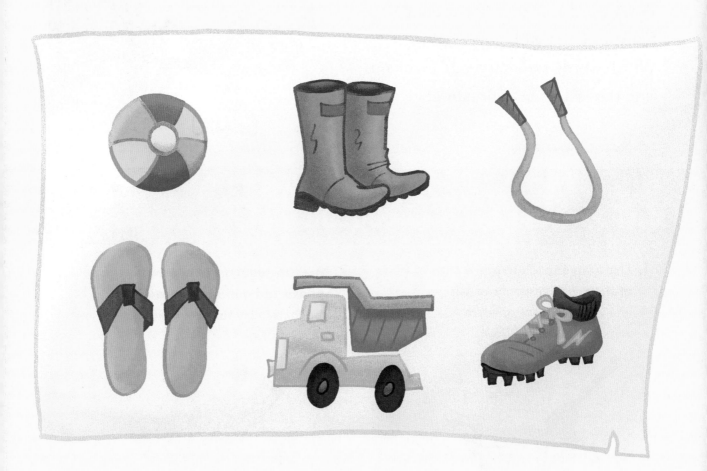

LET'S START! GATHER THESE TOOLS AND MATERIALS.

10 or more craft sticks

Spoon

Flour

Salt

Bowl

Baking tray

Markers

Paper

Modeling clay

LET'S TINKER!

Take a craft stick and go on a word hunt. What words can you find around you? **Point** to them with your stick! Which words can you read? Can you find the letters in your name?

LET'S MAKE: COLOR DICE!

1. Use a large spoon to mix ¼ cup of flour, 2 tablespoons of salt, and 2 tablespoons of warm water together in a bowl.

2. Move the dough to a table with a sprinkle of flour on it. **Knead** the dough like clay for a few minutes.

3. Form a small ball of dough into the shape of a die (a cube). **Press** your thumb into each side to make a small indent. This will help as the dough puffs up in the oven.

4. Put the dough on a baking tray. With the help of an adult, **place** the tray in a 250-degree oven for 1½–3 hours, until the dough is dry and hard.

5. When the dough is cool, **use** markers to color each side of the die a different color.

6. Find a partner to play a game! One player rolls the die and says the name of the color aloud, like red. The other player must run and touch something that is that color, like an apple. **Take turns** rolling and running.

LET'S ENGINEER!

Enid wants to buy raisin buns. But the bridge is closed for repairs!

How can she get over the lake to the bakery?

Trace your hand in the middle of a sheet of paper. **Color** it blue, like Tinker Town's lake. Using your craft sticks and modeling clay, **build** a model of a bridge that could help Enid get over the lake.

PROJECT 8: DONE!
Get your sticker!

Reading Fundamentals

With the help of an adult, sing this song to the tune of *"The Wheels on the Bus."*

The letters join together to spell words,

to spell words,

to spell words.

The letters join together to spell words,

We can spell anything!

What letters join together to spell your name?

Circle each card with a letter.

Underline each card with a word.

Words can be put together to make **sentences**. Words in a sentence are separated by spaces. To read sentences, follow the words from left to right.

Touch the dot under each word while you read each sentence.

I like rain.

I like sun.

I like snow.

Draw a line to match each MotMot to the gear they need to go outside.

To read sentences, start at the top line and move down to the bottom line. When you are done with a page, start again at the top of the next page.

Touch the dot under each word while you read these sentences.

I like red.

I like yellow.

I like green.

I like blue.

I like the rainbow!

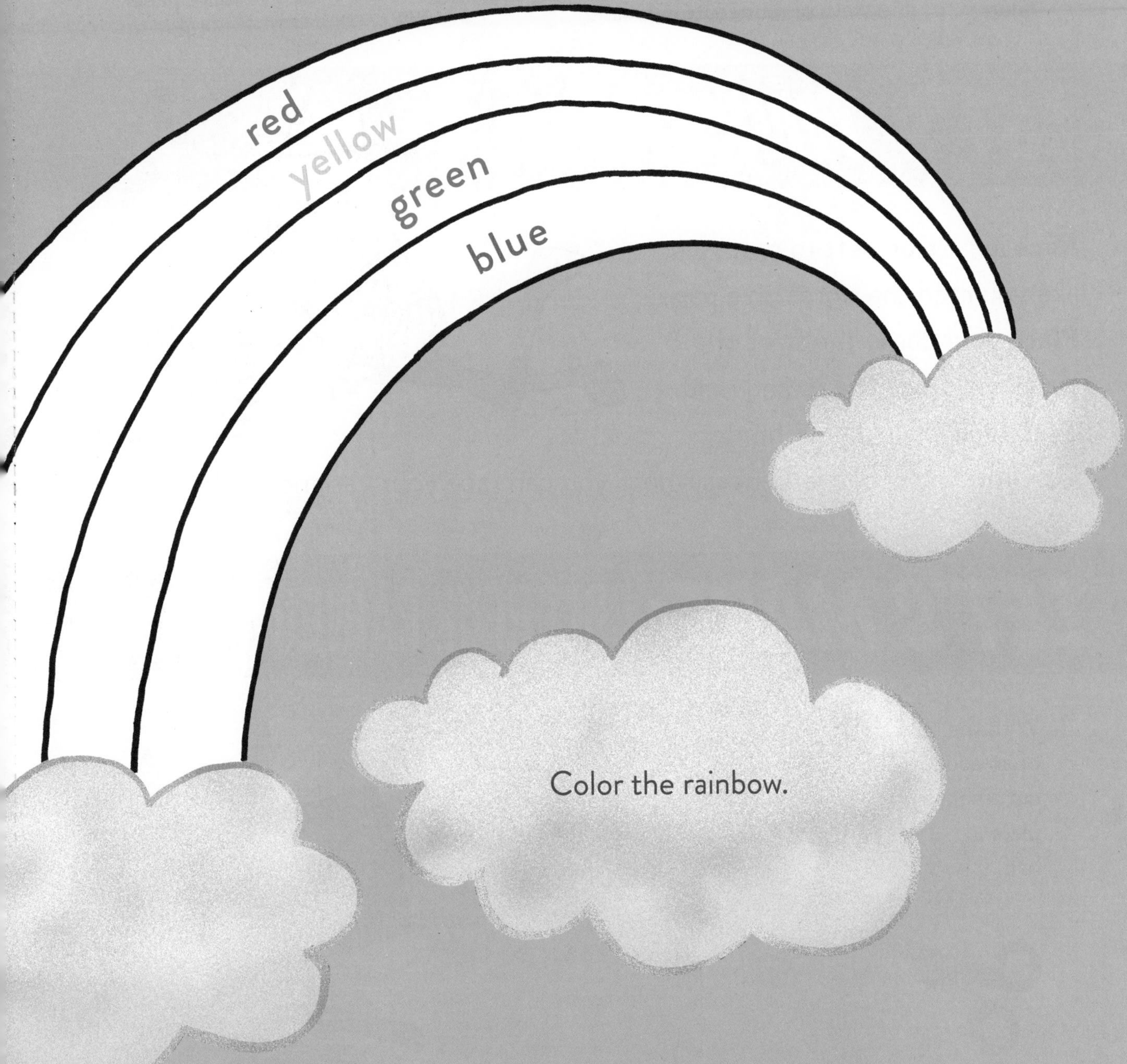

red
yellow
green
blue

Color the rainbow.

Small toy car
(you can also use
a small toy ball)

Scissors
(with an adult's help)

Paper plate

5 or more sheets of
different-colored paper

Glue

15 or more cotton balls

Tape

Toilet paper
tube

LET'S TINKER!

Race a car from left to right, just like you read the words on a page! **Place** your car at the start of a sentence on page 326 and read. Then **look** around your home. Can you find other sentences where you can race your car and read?

LET'S MAKE: COLORFUL RAINBOW!

1. With the help of an adult, **cut** a paper plate in half.

2. With the help of an adult, **cut** a strip from the long side on 5 different-colored sheets of paper.

3. Put a dot of glue on one end of each strip and paste them to the back of the plate at the bottom.

4. Flip the plate over and use glue to attach 15 cotton balls to the front of the plate like a cloud.

LET'S ENGINEER!

Enid is learning that letters join together to form words. Now she's noticing other things that join together to make something new: blocks stack together to make a tower. Dough, tomato sauce, and cheese join together to make pizza.

How can she put her materials together to build something new?

Use your materials to build something new—it could be a rainbow rocket or a racetrack or something completely unique! Which materials will you need? How can you hold the materials together? What colors will you use?

PROJECT 9: DONE!
Get your sticker!

With the help of an adult, read the **newspaper article** aloud.

The Tinker Town News

Fun Fun Friday

Come one, come all, to the most exciting event in Tinker Town: Fun Fun Friday. It is happening today!

In the park you'll see MotMots on the move—leaping, darting, twirling, and grooving. There are games, sports, and races. You can be big or small, quiet or loud, because everyone is welcome. And don't forget—the day ends with a dance party!

We'll see YOU at Fun Fun Friday!

Underline the **tallest** MotMot.
Then circle the **shortest** MotMot.

Quiet and loud are opposites. Opposites are things that are completely different from one another.

Read what each MotMot is doing. Then do the opposite and draw a picture of yourself.

Amelia is pointing **down**. Can you point **up**?

Brian is acting **sad**. Can you act **happy**?

Callie is showing an **open** hand. Can you show a **closed** hand?

Enid and Frank can't wait to dance. Draw a line to lead each MotMot through the maze to the dance party.

Join the dance party! Read each action word, and then act it out.

wiggle

bounce

hop

jump

twist

spin

Circle the move that is your favorite!

The Fun Fun Friday Opposites Game is starting. To win, the MotMots must do the **opposite** of what they are told!

Read each instruction. Color the picture of the MotMot that's doing the opposite. Then do the correct answer yourself!

Jump **far**.

Place a blanket **under** you.

Lay your socks in a **straight** line.

Look **down** and wave.

Hop on something **hard**.

Look in a mirror and **close** your eyes to see the winner of the game!

LET'S START!

GATHER THESE TOOLS AND MATERIALS.

Paper objects like:
paper cups, a shoebox, a cardboard box, toilet paper

1 or more index cards
(or other small pieces of paper)

Markers or crayons

Scissors
(with an adult's help)

Tape

LET'S TINKER!

Let's move! **Create** an obstacle course. **Use** paper cups, a shoebox, a cardboard box, and toilet paper. What can you dance around? What can you jump in? What can you wiggle through?

LET'S MAKE: MOTMOTS ON THE MOVE!

1. Take an index card and draw a straight line a bit below the halfway mark.

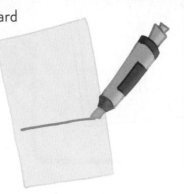

2. On the top of the index card, **draw** the top of your favorite MotMot. You can **add** stickers from page 389.

3. With the help of an adult, **cut** two circles the size of your fingers out of the bottom.

4. Fold the card back on the line and stick your fingers through the holes. They will be the MotMot's legs!

5. Make your MotMot spin, twist, and wiggle. What else can he or she do?

LET'S ENGINEER!

It's Fun Fun Friday, and Amelia has entered the Great Tinker Town Building Game. But all the instructions are written as opposites:

- Build a **short** tower.

- Add **closed** windows.

- Raise a **small** flag.

- Make some flowers **behind** the tower.

How can she figure out what she needs to build to win the game?

Use your materials to build the opposite of each instruction! Can you create a winning tower? Which of your materials can you use to build the tower? How can you add windows, a flag, and flowers?

PROJECT 10: DONE!
Get your sticker!

Point to each picture and tell the story in your own words.

1

2

3

4

Circle the answer to each question.

Who is having a birthday?

What did the octopus make?

Where was the party?

Tell a family member or friend the steps that the octopus took to make the birthday treat!

Point to each picture and tell the story in your own words.

Circle the answer to each question.

Who is hungry?

What did the robot make?

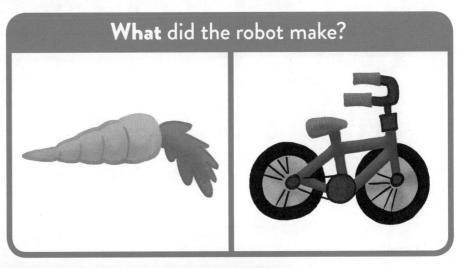

Why was the rabbit happy?

Draw the food
you would order
from the robot.

Point to each picture and tell the story in your own words.

Circle the animals that hid in the tree.
Draw an **X** on the animal that was left out of the tree.

Why didn't this animal hide in the tree? Where could it go
instead? Draw your own ending to the story! Then tell the
story with your new ending to a friend or family member.

LET'S START!

GATHER THESE TOOLS AND MATERIALS.

Crayons or markers

6–10 wooden clothespins

3–4 feet of string

Scissors (with an adult's help)

Empty jar

Piece of newspaper

Fork

Nut or seed butter

Birdseed

Paper

LET'S TINKER!

Use crayons or markers to draw a face on a clothespin. What other details can you add? **Clip** your new friend to your shirt. Where will you go? What will you see? **Tell** a story about your adventures!

LET'S MAKE: PICNIC FOR THE BIRDS!

1. With the help of an adult, **cut** a piece of string about as long as your body.

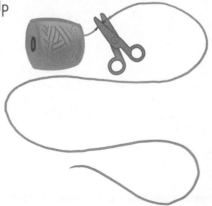

2. Tie it around the top of an empty jar, and put the lid on to hold it in place.

3. Lay a large piece of newspaper down to make a workspace.

4. Use a fork to cover the *outside* of the jar in nut or seed butter.

5. Pour 1 cup of birdseed into the middle of the newspaper. **Roll** the jar in the seeds until it is completely covered.

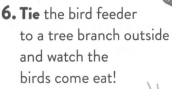

6. Tie the bird feeder to a tree branch outside and watch the birds come eat!

LET'S ENGINEER!

Frank loves telling stories to his friends. But his friends sometimes get confused— they can't see the story, so they don't always understand what is happening.

How can Frank show his friends what happens in his story?

Build your own people and animals to tell your own story! You can **use** paper and clothespins to make them. Then **tell** your story!
Who is in your story? What is he or she doing? Where is he or she going? How does your story end?

PROJECT 11: DONE!
Get your sticker!

With the help of an adult, read this African folktale aloud.

The Caterpillar's Roar

A curious caterpillar saw a cozy cave and crawled inside. Later, a rabbit returned to his cave and saw some strange marks outside in the dirt. He called out, "Who's there?"

The caterpillar was worried about the loud voice outside. So she said, "Me! I am a large beast. I can stomp on an elephant!" Her voice echoed and roared inside the cave—just like a large beast! The rabbit was very afraid.

The rabbit asked his friend the leopard for help. At the cave, the leopard howled, "Who's there?" The caterpillar was worried about the howling. She said, "Me! I am a large beast. I can stomp on an elephant!" Again, her voice echoed and roared. The leopard was very afraid.

A frog hopped over to find out what was wrong. He leaped to the cave and said, "Who's there? I have strong legs and I can jump higher than an elephant!"

The caterpillar was worried about a creature that could jump so high, so she tried to sneak out of the cave. But the rabbit, the leopard, and the frog spotted her! They had been fooled by a tiny caterpillar! They laughed so hard that the caterpillar got away.

A **character** is a person or animal in a story. Cross out two pictures that were not characters in this story.

Draw a line to match the character who lives in the cave to its home.

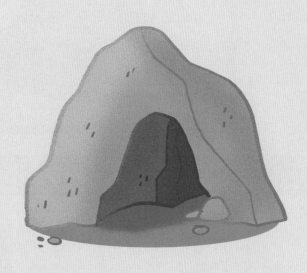

Read the folktale again, and use a different voice for each character.

Circle the answer to each question.

Where did the rabbit live?

Who went inside the rabbit's home?

How did the rabbit know someone was inside his home?

Who was not afraid?

Share ideas with a friend or family member: **Why** wasn't this character afraid?

Point to each picture in order and retell the folktale.
Then color the characters.

1

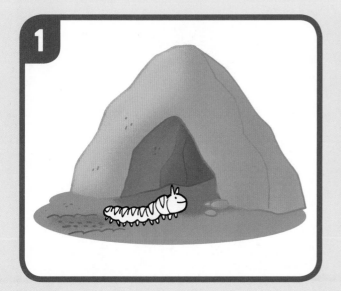

2

3

4

5

6

In the folktale, the characters had many feelings.

The caterpillar was worried.

Draw a picture of a time that you were worried. How did you act?

The frog was surprised.

Draw a picture of a time that you were surprised. How did you act?

Read the folktale again. Talk with a family member about other feelings you hear in the story.

A **setting** is where a story takes place. This folktale takes place at the rabbit's cave.

Make your own cave with a blanket and other items around you. Then act out the story by yourself or with a friend or family member. Draw a picture of you in your setting.

LET'S START!

GATHER THESE TOOLS AND MATERIALS.

½ box cooked and cooled spaghetti

Piece of wax paper

Washable Paint

3 small dishes

Paper

Glue

Small bowl

4 or more pipe cleaners

4 or more craft sticks

LET'S TINKER!

Take a handful of cooked and cooled spaghetti noodles and place them on a piece of wax paper. **Curl** them, roll them, wiggle them, break them apart, and make pictures. What do they feel like? Can you make pictures of any characters? Can you make pictures of any settings?

LET'S MAKE: CATERPILLAR TRACKS!

1. Squeeze 3 colors of paint into 3 small dishes.

2. Drop 1 piece of cooked spaghetti into one color of paint. **Stir** it around with your fingers until it is covered.

3. Pick-up the spaghetti and move it to a piece of paper. **Try** dropping it, rolling it, and dragging it to make caterpillar tracks.

4. Try again with more colors!

LET'S ENGINEER!

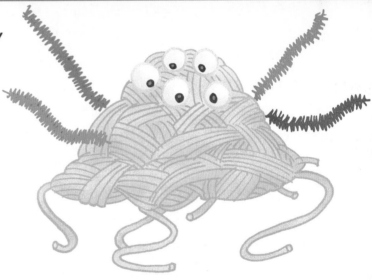

Amelia read a folktale about a very curious monster. The story said, "The monster lurked in the deep waters. You couldn't count its many arms and legs—they swirled all around!"

How can she build a model of the curious monster from the story?

Make a model of your own monster! **Squeeze** about a tablespoon of glue and a tablespoon of paint into the bottom of a small bowl. **Put** a handful (about a cup) of cooked and cooled spaghetti into the bowl and stir with your fingers until the spaghetti is completely covered in the colored glue. **Lift** the spaghetti out and onto a piece of wax paper. **Move** it around to create the head, body, arms, and legs of your monster. What other materials can you add to create more arms and legs? **Add** stickers of eyes and features from page 389 and let your monster dry overnight.

PROJECT 12: DONE!
Get your sticker!

With the help of an adult, read the recipe aloud.

Smiley Bread

1. Gather these ingredients: a piece of bread, nut or seed butter, a banana, and some raisins.

2. Peel the banana and, with the help of an adult, cut three slices.

3. With the help of an adult, use a knife to spread the nut or seed butter onto the bread in a circle.

4. Lay the banana slices and raisins on top to make a face.

Circle the ingredients in Smiley Bread.

Circle the tool that you need.

With the help of an adult, gather these ingredients
and the tool to make Smiley Bread yourself!

Trace the numbers **1**, **2**, **3**, and **4** to put the illustrations in order from first to last. Then point to each illustration in order and retell how to make the recipe.

1

2

3

4

Amelia made her own Smiley Bread.

Find three things that are the same as Brian's and point to them.

Find three things that are different from Brian's and circle them.

Circle the pictures of other recipes Brian can make with these ingredients and tool.

Write and draw your own recipe for Smiley Bread. What ingredients will you use? What kind of face will you make?

Recipe:

_____'s

Smiley Bread

1.

2.

3.

4.

Tell a friend or a family member how to make your recipe!

LET'S START! GATHER THESE TOOLS AND MATERIALS.

 Small objects like: a penny, a cotton ball, a piece of dried pasta, a paper clip, a pinecone, or a rock	 Paper plates	Fork and spoon	English muffin	 Baking tray
Small can or jar of tomato or pizza sauce	½ cup of shredded mozzarella cheese	Optional pizza toppings: pepperoni, peppers, mushrooms, or olives	Modeling clay	

LET'S TINKER!

Flip, roll, stack, and line up your small materials on a paper plate. Can you make faces that are the same and faces that are different? How are they the same and different?

LET'S MAKE: ENID'S MINI PIZZAS!

1. Use a fork to split an English muffin in half.

2. Lay the 2 pieces out on a baking tray with the insides facing up.

3. Spread 1 spoonful of tomato or pizza sauce on each.

4. Sprinkle 2 spoonfuls of shredded mozzarella cheese on each pizza.

5. Add your favorite toppings, like pepperoni, cut-up peppers, mushrooms, or olives.

6. With the help of an adult, **bake** in an oven at 400 degrees for 8–10 minutes.

7. Let the pizzas cool and then enjoy!

LET'S ENGINEER!

Enid loves making her round, Enid-shaped mini pizzas. She wants to make a specially shaped pizza for her friend Frank, too.

How can Enid make a triangular, Frank-shaped pizza?

Read Enid's Mini Pizza recipe. Then **use** modeling clay to build a Frank-shaped model. (You can also ask an adult to cut an English muffin into a triangle, like Frank!)

Show your model to a friend or family member, and explain each step of the new recipe!

PROJECT 13: DONE!
Get your sticker!

Telling a Story

Frank and MotBot had an exciting day. With the help of an adult, read MotBot's diary entry aloud.

> Today I went on a robot walk with my friend Frank. We went to the park. We walked by a pot of flowers, a tall slide, and a water fountain. It started to get dark and we saw the sky turn pink, purple, and orange! Frank called it a "sunset." I was surprised and excited to see it. *Beep beep*!

Have you ever seen a sunset? Tell a friend or family member what it looked like!

Draw a line to lead MotBot through the maze to the water fountain.

Draw a picture of you with your friends. Point to each person and say his or her name aloud.

Add details by drawing the clothes each person is wearing!

Write about and draw one place you like to go with your friends.

Write about and draw one thing you like to do with your friends.

Write and draw your own diary entry about something you did with your family. Where did you go? What did you do?

Ask an adult to help you share your story! You can use computers, tablets, phones, and more.

Write about and draw how you felt. Were you happy,
excited, or nervous?

Ask a family member what he or she remembers about this event.
Write and draw the new details that you learn.

LET'S START!

GATHER THESE TOOLS AND MATERIALS.

Modeling clay

Small objects like:
a penny, dried pasta, a paper clip, a pipe cleaner, a rock,
and small hardware like washers or bolts

Scissors
(with an adult's help)

Construction paper

Tape

Crayons

LET'S TINKER!

Use the modeling clay to design your own MotBot. Then **use** small objects from your materials to add details. What is it wearing? What features does it have?

LET'S MAKE: FINGER PUPPETS!

1. Cut two squares, each about 2 inches by 2 inches, from a piece of construction paper.

2. Wrap one square around your finger, like a tube, and tape it in place. Then **wrap** and tape the next one around another finger.

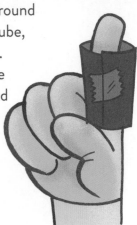

3. Use paper, crayons, and tape to add faces, hair, and accessories to each puppet. You can **create** your own characters or make them look like you and your family (and even your pets!). You can also **add** stickers from page 389.

4. Put the puppets on your fingers and act out your own story.

LET'S ENGINEER!

Amelia and Brian are each telling a story. Amelia's story takes place in a dark cave. Brian's story takes place on top of a volcano. They have only one ball of modeling clay to share.

How can they build one setting that has **both** a dark cave and a high volcano?

Use your modeling clay to build the setting for Amelia's and Brian's stories. How can you create a cave that your finger puppet can go inside? What other materials can you use? How tall can you build the volcano? What other kinds of settings can you build for your finger puppets? What stories can you tell with your characters and settings?

PROJECT 14: DONE!
Get your sticker!

With the help of an adult, read this article aloud.

Zebras

Zebras are amazing animals. In fact, no two zebras have stripes that are the same! So why do zebras have these unique black-and-white stripes? No one knows for sure. Many people believe that the stripes help the animals to mix together as a herd, to protect themselves from predators.

Zebras live in grasslands in Africa. There they eat leaves, twigs, and grasses. They have space to run—and they move fast. Zebras can go up to forty miles per hour. That's much faster than people can run!

Zebras are unique and interesting animals. Keep an eye out for their special stripes in pictures, at the zoo, or in Africa!

Color in the circle below each correct answer.

What colors are zebras?

○ ○ ○

Where do zebras live?

○ ○ ○

What do zebras eat?

○ ○ ○

Write about and draw
your favorite animal.

My Favorite Animal

Point to and label any parts
of the animal that you know!

This animal lives:

on land

in the water

in the sky

◯   ◯   ◯

This animal eats:

This is my favorite animal because:

Act it out: Can you move like this animal? Does it fly, swim, or run?

Ask a friend or family member about their favorite animal.
Write about and draw what you learn.

Friend or family member's name:

Favorite animal:

What does this animal look like?

How does this animal move?

This animal lives:

on land

in the water

in the sky

○   ○   ○

This animal eats:

_____
- - - - - - - - - - - - - - - - -
_____

This is their favorite animal because:

_____
- - - - - - - - - - - - - - - - -
_____

Could their favorite animal meet your favorite animal? What might happen?

LET'S START!

GATHER THESE TOOLS AND MATERIALS.

 Washable Paint	 Paper	Plastic comb	Fork	Construction paper	 Large paper bag
Scissors (with an adult's help)	 Crayons or markers	Glue	3 large square pieces of foil	 Small objects like: pennies, rocks, cotton balls, or paper clips	

LET'S TINKER!

Squeeze a pile of paint into the middle of a piece of paper. **Use** a plastic comb to move the paint. What happens when you tap the comb? What happens when you drag the comb? Can you make stripes like a zebra? **Try** using a fork. How is it the same as the comb, and how is it different? **Try** again using colored paper. What colors of stripes can you make?

LET'S MAKE: ALL ABOUT ME POSTER!

1. With the help of an adult, **cut** the bottom off a paper bag.

2. Then **cut** up one long side. **Lay** the bag open flat to create a large poster.

3. Write your name at the top.

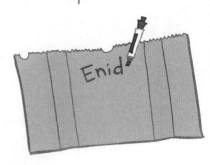

Enid

4. Draw things that mean something to YOU! You could also **cut out** pictures from magazines or photographs and glue them to the poster. **Add** your favorite things, like animals, foods, toys, and games. You could also **add** details about your life, like your family, home, and school. **Try** tracing your hand, or even your head and shoulders!

5. When you are done, **share** the poster with a friend or family member.

LET'S ENGINEER!

Callie's favorite animals are horses. She loves to play with them: She imagines that her toy horses eat grass, sleep in a barn, run, and jump!

How can she build a place for her toy horses to eat, sleep, and play?

Use foil to make models of your own favorite animals. Then **use** your materials to build a place for them to eat, sleep, and play! Do your animals need a tree? A barn? A pool? What about things to play with? When you are finished, **tell** a friend or family member what you made to help take care of your animals!

PROJECT 15: DONE!
Get your sticker!

ANSWER KEY

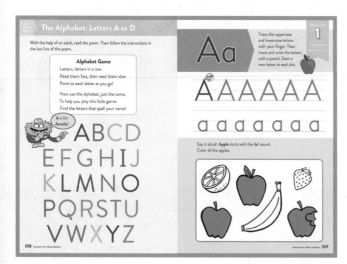

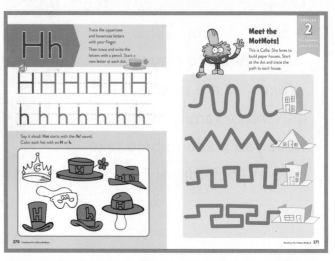

Ii

Trace the uppercase and lowercase letters with your finger. Then trace and write the letters with a pencil. Start a new letter at each dot.

I I I I I I I I

i i i i i i i

Say it aloud: **Igloo** starts with the /i/ sound. Color each block with an **I** or **i**.

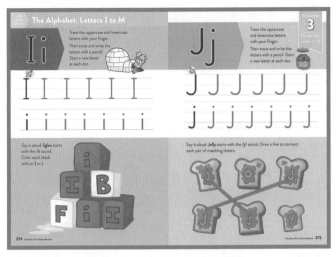

Jj

Trace the uppercase and lowercase letters with your finger. Then trace and write the letters with a pencil. Start a new letter at each dot.

J J J J J J

j j j j j j j

Say it aloud: **Jelly** starts with the /j/ sound. Draw a line to connect each pair of matching letters.

Kk

Trace the uppercase and lowercase letters with your finger. Then trace and write the letters with a pencil. Start a new letter at each dot.

K K K K K K

k k k k k k

Say it aloud: **Kite** starts with the /k/ sound. Color all the kites.

Meet the MotMots!

This is Dimitri. He loves drums. Color each drum that has the letter **D**, like his name.

Ll

Trace the uppercase and lowercase letters with your finger. Then trace and write the letters with a pencil. Start a new letter at each dot.

L L L L L L

l l l l l l l

Say it aloud: **Leaf** starts with the /l/ sound. Say each word aloud. Circle the objects with names that start with the /l/ sound.

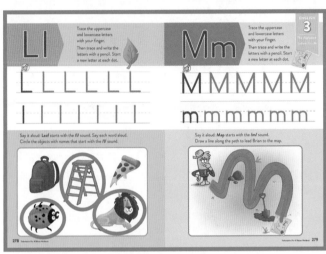

Mm

Trace the uppercase and lowercase letters with your finger. Then trace and write the letters with a pencil. Start a new letter at each dot.

M M M M M

m m m m m m

Say it aloud: **Map** starts with the /m/ sound. Draw a line along the path to lead Brian to the map.

Nn

Trace the uppercase and lowercase letters with your finger. Then trace and write the letters with a pencil. Start a new letter at each dot.

N N N N N

n n n n n n n

Say it aloud: **Nest** starts with the /n/ sound. Circle each nest.

Meet the MotMots!

This is Enid. She loves writing her name. Names begin with capital letters. Trace a capital letter **E** on each of her items.

Oo

Trace the uppercase and lowercase letters with your finger. Then trace and write the letters with a pencil. Start a new letter at each dot.

O O O O O

o o o o o o o

Say it aloud: **Octopus** starts with the /o/ sound. Color all the octopuses.

Pp

Trace the uppercase and lowercase letters with your finger. Then trace and write the letters with a pencil. Start a new letter at each dot.

P P P P P P

p p p p p p p

Say it aloud: **Pig** starts with the /p/ sound. Say the name of each object aloud. Circle the objects with names that start with the /p/ sound.

Meet the MotMots!

This is Frank. He loves animals. Trace the missing letters to complete the name of each animal.

dog   pig

cat   fox

Qq

Trace the uppercase and lowercase letters with your finger. Then trace and write the letters with a pencil. Start a new letter at each dot.

Q Q Q Q Q Q

q q q q q q q

Say it aloud: **Quilt** starts with the /qu/ sound. Draw a line between the matching letters.

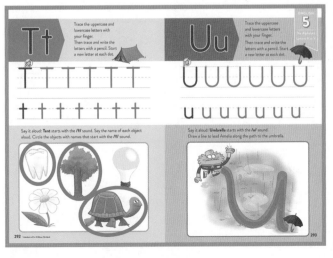

Rr

Trace the uppercase and lowercase letters with your finger. Then trace and write the letters with a pencil. Start a new letter at each dot.

R R R R R R

r r r r r r r

Say it aloud: **Rose** starts with the /r/ sound. Write the missing **R** and color the roses.

Roses

Ss

Trace the uppercase and lowercase letters with your finger. Then trace and write the letters with a pencil. Start a new letter at each dot.

S S S S S S

s s s s s s s s

Say it aloud: **Sock** starts with the /s/ sound. Draw a line to match each snake to its sock.

Tt

Trace the uppercase and lowercase letters with your finger. Then trace and write the letters with a pencil. Start a new letter at each dot.

T T T T T T

t t t t t t t

Say it aloud: **Tent** starts with the /t/ sound. Say the name of each object aloud. Circle the objects with names that start with the /t/ sound.

Uu

Trace the uppercase and lowercase letters with your finger. Then trace and write the letters with a pencil. Start a new letter at each dot.

U U U U U U

u u u u u u u

Say it aloud: **Umbrella** starts with the /u/ sound. Draw a line to lead Amelia along the path to the umbrella.

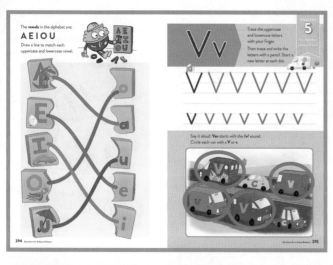

The vowels in the alphabet are:

AEIOU

Draw a line to match each uppercase and lowercase vowel.

V v

Trace the uppercase letters with your finger. Then trace and write the letters with a pencil. Start a new letter at each dot.

VVVVVV

vvvvvv

Say it aloud: **Van** starts with the /v/ sound. Circle each van with a **V** or **v**.

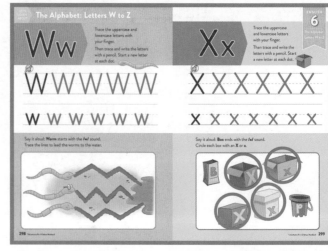

The Alphabet: Letters W to Z

W w

Trace the uppercase and lowercase letters with your finger. Then trace and write the letters with a pencil. Start a new letter at each dot.

WWWWW

wwwww

Say it aloud: **Warm** starts with the /w/ sound. Trace the lines to lead the worms to the water.

X x

Trace the uppercase and lowercase letters with your finger. Then trace and write the letters with a pencil. Start a new letter at each dot.

XXXXXX

xxxxxx

Say it aloud: **Box** ends with the /x/ sound. Circle each box with an **X** or **x**.

Y y

Trace the uppercase and lowercase letters with your finger. Then trace and write the letters with a pencil. Start a new letter at each dot.

YYYYYY

yyyyyy

Say it aloud: **Yo-yo** starts with the /y/ sound. Color all the yo-yos.

Z z

Trace the uppercase and lowercase letters with your finger. Then trace and write the letters with a pencil. Start a new letter at each dot.

ZZZZZZ

zzzzzz

Say it aloud: **Zipper** starts with the /z/ sound. Draw a line to move the zipper to the bottom.

Draw a line to lead Enid along the path from the ape to the zebra. Start at the letter **A**. Say the name of each letter aloud as you go.

Use the letters of the alphabet to spell your name. Write an uppercase letter for the first letter, like this:

Frank

Answers will vary.

Write your name on each item.

Answers will vary.

Answers will vary.

Phonics

Rhyming words have middle and ending sounds that are the same. Frank's best friend MotBot loves rhyming words—even he name rhymes! Read each pair of rhyming words and trace the middle and ending sounds.

pat a cat

hop on top

hug a bug

run for fun

Say the name of each pair of objects aloud, and color the pairs that rhyme.

dog   log

Answers will vary.

pup   cup

Answers will vary.

pen   bed

pig   wig

Answers will vary.

Brian's favorite letter is **B**. He likes balls and boats! Point to each picture below and say the object's name aloud. Circle the objects that start with the /b/ sound.

Trace the first letter of each word with a pencil and read the word aloud. Then draw a line to match each word to its picture.

bat

cat

hat

rat

Point to something you see near you that starts with the letter **B**.

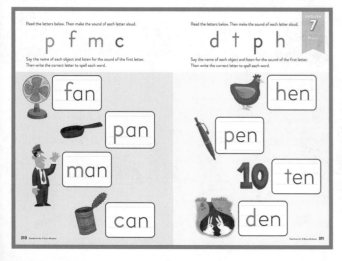

Read the letters below. Then make the sound of each letter aloud.

p f m c

Say the name of each object and listen for the sound of the first letter. Then write the correct letter to spell each word.

fan

pan

man

can

Read the letters below. Then make the sound of each letter aloud.

d t p h

Say the name of each object and listen for the sound of the first letter. Then write the correct letter to spell each word.

hen

pen

ten

den

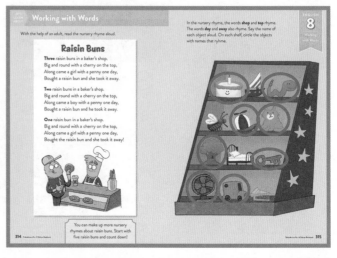

Working with Words

With the help of an adult, read the nursery rhyme aloud.

Raisin Buns

Three raisin buns in a baker's shop.
Big and round with a cherry on the top,
Along came a girl with a penny one day,
Bought a raisin bun and she took it away.

Two raisin buns in a baker's shop.
Big and round with a cherry on the top,
Along came a boy with a penny one day,
Bought a raisin bun and he took it away.

One raisin bun in a baker's shop.
Big and round with a cherry on the top,
Along came a girl with a penny one day,
Bought the raisin bun and she took it away!

You can make up more nursery rhymes about raisin buns. Start with five raisin buns and count down!

In the nursery rhyme, the words **shop** and **top** rhyme. The words **day** and **away** also rhyme. Say the name of each object aloud. On each shelf, circle the objects with names that rhyme.

Amelia sees a lot of words on her way to the bakery. With the help of an adult, point to each word and read it aloud. Then color the signs.

Answers will vary.

BUS · STOP · WALK · FLOWERS · FISH · BOOKS · BAKERY · Milk

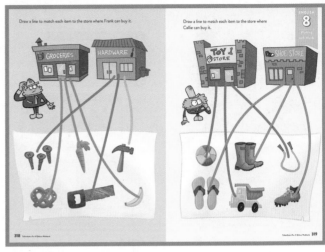

Draw a line to match each item to the store where Frank can buy it.

Draw a line to match each item to the store where Callie can buy it.

GROCERIES · HARDWARE · TOY STORE · SHOE STORE

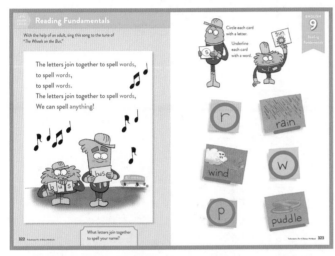

Reading Fundamentals

With the help of an adult, sing this song to the tune of "The Wheels on the Bus."

The letters join together to spell words,
to spell words,
to spell words.
The letters join together to spell words,
We can spell anything!

What letters join together to spell your name?

Circle each card with a letter.
Underline each card with a word.

r · rain · wind · W · P · puddle

Words can be put together to make sentences. Words in a sentence are separated by spaces. To read sentences, follow the words from left to right.

Touch the dot under each word while you read each sentence.

I like rain.

I like sun.

I like snow.

Draw a line to match each MotMot to the gear they need to go outside.

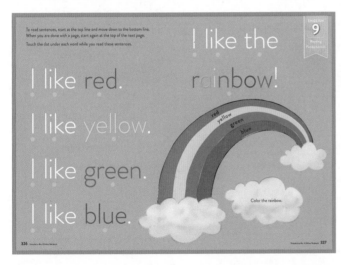

To read sentences, start at the top line and move down to the bottom line. When you are done with a page, start again at the top of the next page. Touch the dot under each word while you read these sentences.

I like red.

I like yellow.

I like green.

I like blue.

I like the rainbow!

red · yellow · green · blue

Color the rainbow.

Vocabulary

With the help of an adult, read the newspaper article aloud.

The Tinker Town News

Fun Fun Friday

Come one, come all, to the most exciting event in Tinker Town: Fun Fun Friday. It is happening today!

In the park you'll see MotMots on the move—leaping, darting, twirling, and grooving. There are games, sports, and races. You can be big or small, quiet or loud, because everyone is welcome. And don't forget—the day ends with a dance party!

We'll see YOU at Fun Fun Friday!

Underline the tallest MotMot. Then circle the shortest MotMot.

Quiet and loud are opposites. Opposites are things that are completely different from one another.

Read what each MotMot is doing. Then do the opposite and draw a picture of yourself.

Amelia is pointing down. Can you point up?

Answers will vary.

Answers will vary.

Brian is acting sad. Can you act happy?

Callie is showing an open hand. Can you show a closed hand?

Answers will vary.

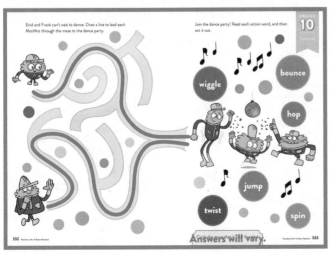

Enid and Frank can't wait to dance. Draw a line to lead each MotMot through the maze to the dance party.

Join the dance party! Read each action word, and then act it out.

wiggle · bounce · hop · jump · twist · spin

Answers will vary.

The Fun Fun Friday Opposites Game is starting. To win, the MotMots must do the opposite of what they are told!

Read each instruction. Color the picture of the MotMot that's doing the opposite. Then do the correct answer yourself!

Jump far.

Look down and wave.

Place a blanket under you.

Hop on something hard.

Lay your socks in a straight line.

Look in a mirror and close your eyes to see the winner of the game!

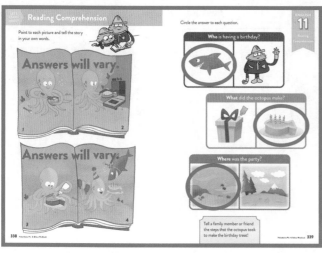
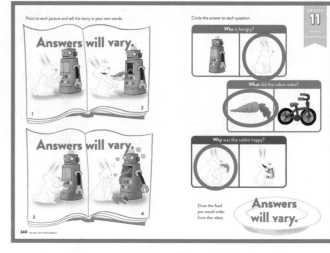

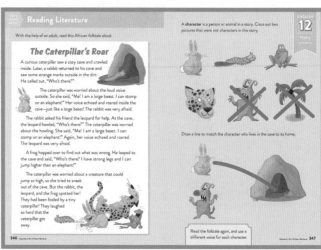
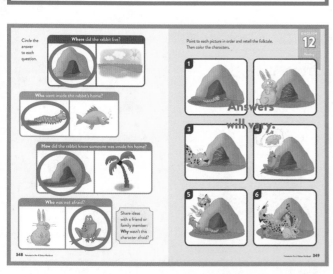
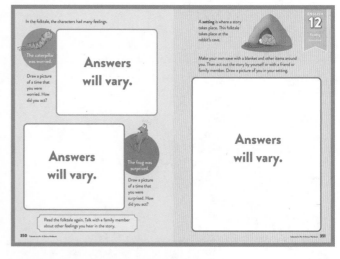

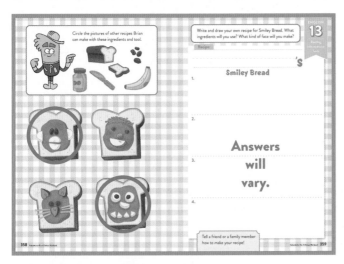

Circle the pictures of other recipes Brian can make with these ingredients and tool.

Write and draw your own recipe for Smiley Bread. What ingredients will you use? What kind of face will you make?

Recipe:

_____'s

Smiley Bread

1.

2. Answers will vary.

3.

4.

Tell a friend or a family member how to make your recipe!

ENGLISH 13

ENGLISH 14

Telling a Story

Frank and MotBot had an exciting day. With the help of an adult, read MotBot's diary entry aloud.

Today I went on a robot walk with my friend Frank. We went to the park. We walked by a pot of flowers, a tall slide, and a water fountain. It started to get dark and we saw the sky turn pink, purple, and orange! Frank called it a "sunset." I was surprised and excited to see it. Beep beep!

Have you ever seen a sunset? Tell a friend or family member what it looked like!

Draw a line to lead MotBot through the maze to the water fountain.

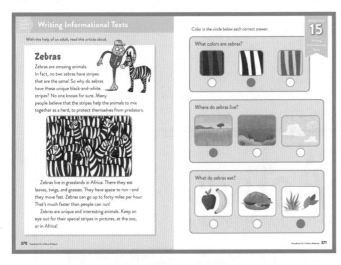

Draw a picture of you with your friends. Point to each person and say his or her name aloud.

Answers will vary.

Add details by drawing the clothes each person is wearing!

Write about and draw one place you like to go with your friends.

Answers will vary.

Write about and draw one thing you like to do with your friends.

Answers will vary.

ENGLISH 14

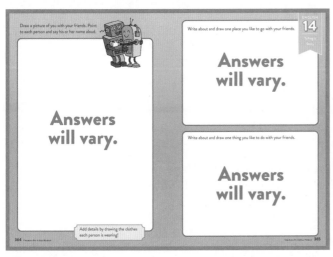

Write and draw your own diary entry about something you did with your family. Where did you go? What did you do?

Answers will vary.

Ask an adult to help you share your story! You can use computers, tablets, phones, and more.

Write about and draw how you felt. Were you happy, excited, or nervous?

Answers will vary.

Ask a family member what he or she remembers about this event. Write and draw the new details that you learn.

Answers will vary.

ENGLISH 14

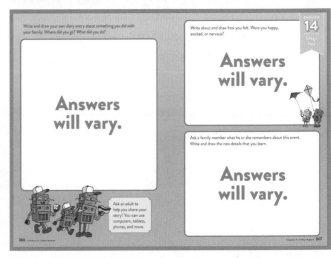

Writing Informational Texts

With the help of an adult, read this article aloud.

Zebras

Zebras are amazing animals. In fact, no two zebras have stripes that are the same! So why do zebras have these unique black-and-white stripes? No one knows for sure. Many people believe that the stripes help the animals to mix together as a herd, to protect themselves from predators.

Zebras live in grasslands in Africa. There they eat leaves, twigs, and grasses. They have space to run—and they move fast. Zebras can go up to forty miles per hour. That's much faster than people can run!

Zebras are unique and interesting animals. Keep an eye out for their special stripes in pictures, at the zoo, or in Africa!

Color in the circle below each correct answer.

What colors are zebras?

Where do zebras live?

What do zebras eat?

ENGLISH 15

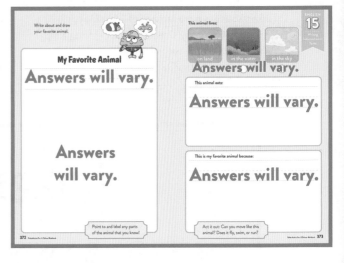

Write about and draw your favorite animal.

My Favorite Animal
Answers will vary.

Answers will vary.

Point to and label any parts of the animal that you know!

This animal lives:
on land   in the water   in the sky
Answers will vary.

This animal eats:
Answers will vary.

This is my favorite animal because:
Answers will vary.

Act it out: Can you move like this animal? Does it fly, swim, or run?

ENGLISH 15

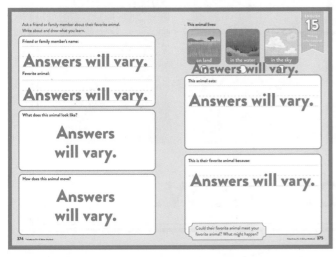

Ask a friend or family member about their favorite animal. Write about and draw what you learn.

Friend or family member's name:
Answers will vary.

Favorite animal:
Answers will vary.

What does this animal look like?
Answers will vary.

How does this animal move?
Answers will vary.

This animal lives:
on land   in the water   in the sky
Answers will vary.

This animal eats:
Answers will vary.

This is their favorite animal because:
Answers will vary.

Could their favorite animal meet your favorite animal? What might happen?

ENGLISH 15

Odd Dot
120 Broadway
New York, NY 10271
OddDot.com

ISBN: 978-1-250-88600-2

WRITERS   Nathalie Le Du and Megan Hewes Butler

ILLUSTRATORS   Les McClaine, Chad Thomas, and Pat Lewis

EDUCATIONAL CONSULTANT   Randi House

CHARACTER DESIGNER   Anna-Maria Jung

LEAD SERIES DESIGNER   Carolyn Bahar

INTERIOR DESIGNERS   Colleen AF Venable, Tim Hall, and Phil Conigliaro

COVER DESIGNER   Caitlyn Hunter

EDITORS   Nathalie Le Du and Kate Avino

Our books may be purchased in bulk for promotional, educational, or business use. Please contact your local bookseller or the Macmillan Corporate and Premium Sales Department at (800) 221-7945 ext. 5442 or by email at MacmillanSpecialMarkets@macmillan.com.

TinkerActive is a trademark of Odd Dot.
Printed in China by Dream Colour (Hong Kong) Printing Limited, Guangdong Province
First published for special markets in 2022
First trade edition, 2023

10 9 8 7 6 5 4 3 2 1

Here's your
TINKERACTIVE MATH EXPERT
sticker!

For the
activity
on page
46

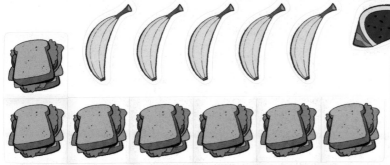

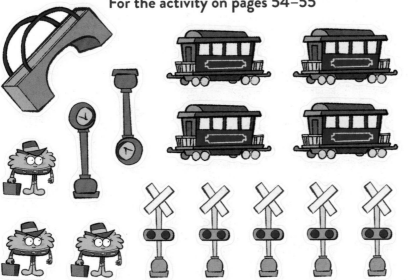

For the activity on
page 79

For the activity on pages 54–55

For the activity on page 105

For the activity on page 101

Sticker your **TINKERACTIVE EXPERT** poster after you
complete each project.

385

For the activity on page 183

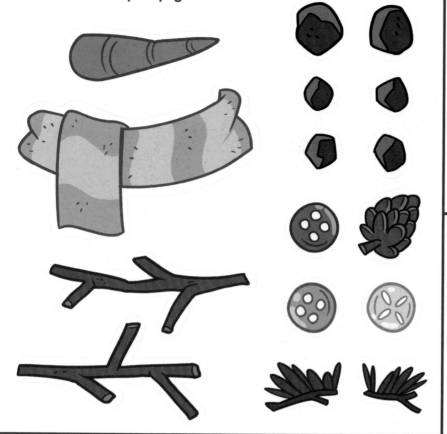

For the activity on page 229

For the activity on page 225

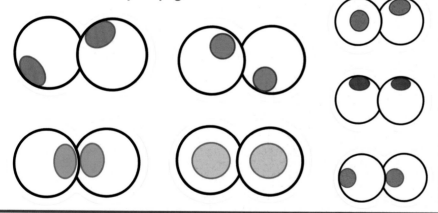

Sticker your *TINKERACTIVE EXPERT* poster after you complete each project.

For the activity on page 289

For the activity on page 336

Here's your
TINKERACTIVE ENGLISH EXPERT sticker!

For the activity on pages 368–369

Sticker your *TINKERACTIVE EXPERT* poster after you complete each project.

For the activity on page 353